CULTURES OF THE WORLD®

SWEDEN

Delice Gan/Leslie Jermyn

BENCHMARK BOOKS

MARSHALL CAVENDISH
NEW YORK

PICTURE CREDITS
Cover photo: © Trip/A. Tovy
AFP: 34, 35, 43, 54, 99, 102 • Art Directors & Trip: 1, 3, 6, 9, 15, 30, 40, 48, 49, 50, 53, 55, 56, 59, 68, 72, 78, 79, 89, 101, 110, 118, 119, 123, 133 • Bes Stock: 52, 57 • Jan Butchofsky/ Houserstock: 58, 91 • Camera Press: 94 • Embassy of Sweden: 25, 33 • Getty Images/Hulton Archive: 19, 28 • Haga Library: 16, 86, 116, 128 • Dave G. Houser/Houserstock: 5, 14, 51, 77, 90, 95, 97 • IKEA: 130, 131 • Klingwalls Foto: 60, 71, 76, 84, 100, 105, 121, 122 • Life File Photographic Library: 4, 42, 45, 114 • Bosse Lind: 104 • Lonely Planet Images: 23, 31, 61, 92, 107, 108, 125 • MacQuitty International Collection: 81 • Mark Markefelt: 8, 17, 47, 69, 120, 124 • Svenskt Pressfoto: 3, 7, 10, 11, 12, 13, 27, 29, 36, 38, 41, 46, 64, 65, 66, 67, 73, 74, 75, 83, 96, 103, 109, 111, 113, 115, 117, 126, 129 • Swedish Tourism Board: 20 • Topham Picturepoint: 62

ACKNOWLEDGMENTS
With thanks to Paul Norlen for his reading of this manuscript

PRECEDING PAGE
Young folk dancers in traditional dress wait to perform at a competition in Stockholm.

Marshall Cavendish Corporation
99 White Plains Road
Tarrytown, NY 10591
Website: www.marshallcavendish.com

Originated and designed by
Times Books International, an imprint of
Times Media Private Limited, a member of
Times International Publishing

Printed in Singapore

Library of Congress Cataloging-in-Publication Data:
Gan, Delice, 1954–
    Sweden / by Delice Gan and Leslie Jermyn.—2nd ed.
        p. cm.—(Cultures of the world)
    Summary: Introduces the geography, history, economy, culture, and people of the fourth largest country in Europe.
    Includes bibliographical references and index.
    ISBN 0-7614-1502-5
    1. Sweden—Juvenile literature. [1. Sweden.] I. Jermyn, Leslie. II. Title. III. Series.
DL609.G36 2003
948.5—dc21   2002152559

7 6 5 4 3

CONTENTS

Swedish children dressed in warm clothes enjoy the outdoors in the winter.

Flowers brighten up a town square.

INTRODUCTION

SWEDEN IS A LAND of lakes and seas, mountains and plains, industry and agriculture. It has a long history that includes Viking voyages and wonderful arts. Some uniquely Swedish personalities and products are world-famous: film director Ingmar Bergman, actress Ingrid Bergman, Alfred Nobel and the international prizes he established, Pippi Longstocking from Astrid Lindgren's children's books, the car brands Volvo and Saab, furniture maker Ikea, the Hasselblad camera (a favorite of professional photographers), and of course, the meatball.

Swedes love the outdoors and are great sportspeople. They are also peace-loving; they have remained neutral in conflicts since the 19th century. With their high standard of living and commitment to human rights and environmental protection, Swedes are a model for the rest of the world to follow. This book explores both the country and the character of Sweden, land of the midnight sun.

GEOGRAPHY

SWEDEN IS ONE OF THE northernmost countries in the world; one-seventh of Sweden lies within the Arctic Circle. The country has a long, narrow shape, extending 977 miles (1,572 km) from north to south, and 310 miles (499 km) from west to east.

Sweden is also Europe's fourth largest country, with an area of 173,730 square miles (449,613 square km). This makes it only slightly larger than the U.S. state of California. Sweden's neighbor to the west is Norway, while to the east lies the Gulf of Bothnia and the Baltic Sea. Finland is located in the east across the Gulf of Bothnia, and Denmark lies to the south.

Below: **In the winter, heavy snowfall blankets the countryside.**

Opposite: **Rolling fields in Skåne, a beautiful region in southern Sweden.**

7

REGIONS

Sweden has a varied landscape of mountains, forests, rolling hills, lakes, and expansive plains. Much of the Swedish landscape was shaped during the last Ice Age, 10,000 years ago. Massive glaciers sculpted mountains, lakes, and sandy ridges and fertilized the soil of the central plains with finely ground material left behind as they retreated.

The Kölen Mountains, which run from north to south, form the backbone of the Scandinavian peninsula and act as a natural border between Sweden and Norway. Traditionally, Sweden is divided into three regions: Götaland, Svealand, and Norrland.

At 6,926 feet (2,111 m), Kebnekaise is Sweden's highest mountain.

GÖTALAND The southernmost part of Sweden, called Götaland ("YUE-tah-land"), includes the county of Skåne, whose fertile plains are in fact a continuation of the flat lands of Denmark and northern Germany. The rest of Götaland is broken up by hills, lakes, and lowlands. The island of Öland, in the Baltic Sea, is also part of Götaland.

SVEALAND Svealand ("SVEE-ah-land") refers to Sweden's central region, although it is actually in the southern part of the country. This region has hills, lowland plains, forests, and large river valleys. Sweden's capital, Stockholm, and second largest city, Göteborg (also called Gothenburg), are in Svealand. The island of Gotland, in the Baltic Sea, also forms part of Sweden's central region.

NORRLAND Sweden's northern region, called Norrland ("NOR-land"), covers three-fifths of the country, yet it is only sparsely populated. Norrland is an important mining and forestry region. Sweden's oldest industrial region, Bergslagen, just north of Svealand, was founded on rich deposits of iron and other ores. Copper, lead, and zinc are mined in Västerbotten county.

The Arctic Circle crosses the Lappland region of Sweden's Sami. The country's highest peaks, Mount Kebnekaise at 6,926 feet (2,111 m) and Mount Sarektjåkkå at 6,857 feet (2,090 m), are in Lappland.

A forest in Svealand.

THE GÖTA CANAL AND 100,000 LAKES

The Göta Canal is a major waterway in Sweden. The 55-mile (88.5-km) canal was an amazing civil engineering achievement when it was completed in 1832, linking the industrial city of Göteborg on the western coast to the Baltic Sea. The first part of the canal links Lake Vänern and Lake Vättern, from where it links up with other smaller lakes before reaching the Baltic Sea.

Sweden has almost 100,000 lakes that cover 8.6 percent of its land area. The largest, Lake Vänern in central Sweden, is also Western Europe's largest lake; Vänern covers 3,468 square miles (8,975 square km). Much of Sweden's early industrial development took place north of this lake. In southern Sweden are other large lakes such as Vättern, Mälaren, and Hjälmaren.

Sweden's lakes are fed by rivers flowing from the mountains toward the sea. Many of the rivers have been successfully used to generate hydroelectric power for industrial and urban development. Swedish expertise in hydroelectricity has been exported to other countries.

LAND OF THE MIDNIGHT SUN

Sweden has mild weather compared to other places on the same latitude (around 60° north of the equator), such as Alaska. Sweden's temperatures are moderated by the Gulf Stream and by warm westerly winds blowing in from the North Atlantic Ocean.

In July, the warmest month, average temperatures range from 14°C to 22°C (57°F to 71°F) in Stockholm and 12°C to 21°C (53°F to 69° F) in the northern city of Piteå.

Although winter temperatures vary considerably from north to south, Sweden generally experiences average temperatures below freezing in February, the coldest month, when average temperatures range from -5°C to -1°C (22°F to 30°F) in Stockholm and -14°C to -6°C (6°F to 22°F) in Piteå.

In the south, snow covers the ground from December to March, while northern areas have snow cover from mid-October through mid-April.

In the summer, there is little difference in the weather between the north and south, as Norrland warms up as much as the south due to the long days.

Sweden's arctic zone experiences about two months of continuous twilight in the winter and two months of continuous daylight in the summer. Long summer days and winter nights in this part of the world result from the tilt of the earth's axis as it rotates around the sun. Even in Stockholm, summer nights can be bright, with only a few hours of semi-darkness. This is why Sweden is called the Land of the Midnight Sun.

Overall the weather is milder in the southern coastal areas, which enjoy a longer fall and an earlier spring. Spring may arrive in the southern county of Skåne in February, while the northern region of Lappland may only see the end of winter in late May.

The sun at midnight in the summer.

FLORA AND FAUNA

Forests cover about 68 percent of Sweden's land area and represent just under 1 percent of the world's dense forests. Most of Sweden's forests are found in the northern temperate coniferous belt.

Common to most of the forests are spruce and pine trees, although linden, ash, maple, birch, and aspen are also found. Flowering plants, such as orchids and rock roses, are found in parts of the mountain range and on the islands of Gotland and Öland.

Sweden's fauna has been affected by climate changes since the last Ice Age and also by human settlement. Bears and lynx roam the northern forests, while large numbers of roe deer, moose, hare, and fox are found throughout the country. Motorists often have to stop for moose crossing roads in the forest; traffic signs that read "Danger—Moose" are common on country roads.

The government and the industrial sector work together to replant trees on logged land. Sweden today has more trees in the countryside than ever before.

In the winter, many birds leave Sweden for warmer places, while in the summer, migratory birds fly in from as far away as Egypt and southern Africa. Bird lovers in the countryside have a chance to spot species such as the rare white-tailed eagle, the wild swan, and the redshank.

Sweden is also home to furry, brown rodents called lemmings. One unusual characteristic of lemming behavior is that every few years, they go through a cycle of mass suicides—they migrate in groups to the coast, where they jump into the sea and drown.

Sweden's long coastline and many lakes are home to a rich variety of aquatic life. Fish include cod and mackerel from the salty Atlantic and salmon and pike from the less saline waters of the Gulf of Bothnia and the lakes and rivers. Traditional food staples include herring such as the *strömming* ("STROHM-ming") species from the Baltic. Unfortunately, pollution has threatened the survival of much of Sweden's marine life, endangering certain species, such as the Baltic seal.

To protect the fauna, hunting and fishing are strictly regulated. The government has set aside 20 areas of natural beauty for preservation as national parks. Sweden was the first nation in Europe to establish national parks in 1910. The largest and most famous park in Sweden is Sareks National Park in the Lappland region.

Sweden is famous for its reindeer. Not many reindeer still roam wild; herds are bred on farms for their meat. Most reindeer farms are found in Norrland, especially in the Lappland region.

CROWDED SOUTH, EMPTY NORTH

More than 85 percent of Sweden's 8.9 million people live in the south, which has fertile land and a mild climate. The most densely populated areas are within the triangle formed by the three largest urban centers of Stockholm, Göteborg, and Malmö. These cities hold about a third of Sweden's population. Fewer people live in the north. Norrland has only six persons per square mile (two persons per square km).

STOCKHOLM Stockholm is surrounded by water. It extends across 14 islands and portions of the mainland and spreads across the freshwater Lake Mälaren and Lake Saltsjön, which connects to the city's archipelago and the Baltic Sea. The fresh and salt water are separated by the island of the old city, Gamla Stan, and great artificial canals at the southern end.

The island of Gamla Stan sits in the middle of canals and waterways in the old section of Stockholm.

An oil tanker docked at Göteborg harbor.

Stockholm is also Sweden's most important commercial center; more than one-quarter of the labor force works in Greater Stockholm. The urban area spreads over 250 square miles (647 square km), so it is not crowded. Reflecting typical Swedish concern for the environment, the waters around the city are kept clean and are filled with fish. It is common to see anglers fishing for their dinner right in the heart of the city. In the summer it is popular for leisure activities, with many summer homes on the islands.

GÖTEBORG With 467,000 inhabitants, Göteborg is the country's most important port and also an important industrial center for Sweden's aerospace, automotive, and other engineering industries.

MALMÖ With a population of 259,000, Malmö is an important port. Among the local industries are shipbuilding and automotive production. Located in Sweden's most fertile agricultural region, Malmö also exports agricultural products.

HISTORY

THE FIRST SIGNS of human habitation in Sweden date back to about 10,000 years before the birth of Christ. Stone Age hunters came to Scandinavia as the ice covering the region began to melt. From around 8000 to 6000 B.C., hunters and fishers started to populate the area.

EARLY INHABITANTS

Archeologists have found stone tools that were used during the Bronze Age from 1800 to 500 B.C. Excavations have uncovered bronze weapons and religious artifacts that indicate a high level of culture. This is especially evident in artifacts found in the graves of the period.

The next period, the Iron Age, from 500 B.C. to A.D. 400, saw the beginning of a more settled population and an agriculture-based society.

The development of such a society continued over the period of the great migrations from A.D. 400 to 500 and over the Vendel period from A.D. 550 to 800. The Vendel period is named for the discovery of splendid boat graves at Vendel in the region of Uppland, where the Svea tribe settled. It is from this tribe that the name Sverige or Sweden originated.

In the sixth century, the warring Sveas began to exert their influence over their neighbors. A series of minor wars occured, and by the beginning of the Viking Era in A.D. 800, the Sveas had expanded beyond their original seat of power at Lake Mälaren.

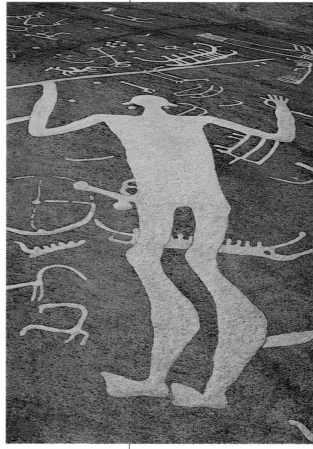

Above: **Rock carvings in the region of Tanum.**

Opposite: **An ancient runestone.**

17

THE VIKINGS

The Viking era lasted from A.D. 800 to 1050. Although this was a relatively short time, the Vikings are still remembered throughout Europe today.

The Vikings sailed from their home bases in Sweden, Norway, and Denmark in longships, attacking other countries across the length and breadth of Europe. The first recorded Viking raid took place in the late eighth century. It was an attack on a rich abbey at Lindisfarne on the northeastern coast of England.

As a result, people described Vikings as barbarians who killed monks and burned books. The Vikings were fierce warriors who showed their enemies no mercy, and they acquired such a ferocious reputation that in many parts of Europe, people prayed, "From the fury of the Norsemen, Good Lord deliver us." Viking warriors showed little fear in battle. They believed that if they died in battle, their souls would go to Valhalla, palace of Odin and the gods. This was their equivalent of heaven.

The Vikings were known not only for plundering but also for trade and expansionism. Vikings from Sweden swept east along the Baltic coast and down along rivers leading to Russia. They set up trading stations and principalities in Russia, like that of the grand prince Rurik at Novgorod. They also went as far as the Black and Caspian seas, where they formed trade links with the Byzantine empire and the Arab states. Some of these Vikings even remained in Byzantium (Constantinople) as members of an elite imperial guard.

Around the 10th century, Vikings from Sweden founded the city of Kiev in Russia as a result of profitable trade in furs, honey, and amber. These travelers also took home precious metals like gold and silver, and luxury goods such as cloth. These goods and artifacts such as coins from Arabia have been found at the site of Sweden's first city, Birka, on the island of

Björkö on Lake Mälaren. This fertile island was the first center of power in Sweden. Today, the nation's capital also lies on this important lake.

Vikings from Denmark raided western Europe, while the Norwegian Vikings expanded west to Britain, Iceland, and Greenland. One famous Viking, Erik the Red, left Norway for Iceland. Exiled from Iceland, he took his family to Greenland, where he raised his sons, Leif, Thorvald, and Thorstein, and daughter, Freydis.

Around A.D. 1000, Leif became the first European to reach North America when he landed on the coast of Vinland (present-day northern Newfoundland). Thorvald later took the same route to Vinland, where he was killed in battle.

The name Viking comes from an old word *vik* ("vick"), meaning bay or creek, places where the Vikings kept their famous longships. The Vikings were excellent sailors, skilled in shipbuilding. Their longships were strong enough to sail in stormy seas, and the boats' round-bottomed hulls allowed them to beach for surprise attacks.

EARLY CHRISTIANITY

Christianity came in the ninth century after the Vikings drew attention to their northern homeland through their expeditions. It arrived through Ansgar, a Benedictine monk. He succeeded in converting some of the inhabitants.

However, in spite of Ansgar's efforts and the efforts of others, Viking religious beliefs and practices persisted. The old Viking religion, with the gods Odin (god of wisdom), Thor (god of thunder), and Frey (god of fertility), continued to be observed by some well into the following century. Viking customs varied from one region to another; some even involved human sacrifice.

Christianity slowly gained ground in the 10th and 11th centuries. Olaf Skötkonung was the first Swedish monarch to be baptized, and an archbishopric was established at Uppsala. By the mid-12th century, when King Erik Jedvarsson converted to Christianity, paganism was no longer practiced and Sweden became a Christian country. King Erik was later canonized as Saint Erik and became the patron saint of Sweden.

UNITING A KINGDOM

Although Sweden became unified in A.D. 1000, the monarchy was still not the central authority. Each province had its own assembly and laws.

After 1250 a new family dynasty called Folkung ruled Sweden. The Folkung was more successful in controlling the provinces. Its first administrator was Birger Jarl, who founded Stockholm and at the same time issued national laws.

In 1280 his son Magnus Ladulås introduced a form of feudalism. A council of nobles and church officials was established to advise the king. The farmers, however, held on to their ancient rights and prevented the implementation of a full feudal system. These ancient rights, which had been handed down orally and were first put into written form in this period, formed Europe's oldest body of written law. By the mid-14th century, a code of law for the whole country was established during the reign of King Magnus Eriksson.

THE HANSEATIC PERIOD

In the 14th century, trade in the Baltic flourished under the leadership of the Hanseatic League, an association of German towns. Sweden also benefited from trade with the Hanseatic League, and the town of Visby on the island of Gotland became an important trading post.

Sweden's economy prospered, and many new towns were founded. German influence spread to the political, social, and cultural spheres. Even the language assimilated many linguistic forms from the German spoken by the Hanseatic traders. However, in spite of enhanced trading activity, agriculture remained the basis of the economy and developed through improved methods and tools.

After a plague killed one-third of the population in the mid-14th century, Sweden's economy collapsed, as many farms were abandoned. It only recovered in the second half of the 15th century when iron production played a more important role in the economy.

Between 1347 and 1351, a terrible outbreak of bubonic plague ravaged Europe. Called the Black Death, it quickly spread across Europe, carried by infected rats, and plunged Scandinavia into devastation.

Opposite: **Dressed as Vikings, these Swedes are celebrating Medieval Week in the town of Visby, an important trading post during the rule of the Hanseatic League. Medieval Week is held in August every year.**

UNION WITH DENMARK

In 1389 the Swedish royal council elected Queen Margrethe of Denmark as ruler of Sweden. Margrethe was an intelligent, astute queen. In 1397 a treaty called the Union of Kalmar united Denmark, Norway, and Sweden under the rule of one crown.

At this time, Denmark was the most advanced of the Scandinavian countries. However, after Margrethe's death, there were conflicts between the monarchy, the nobility, and Sweden's heavily taxed farmers.

In 1435 Margrethe's successor, Erik of Pomerania, was deposed in a revolt led by Engelbrekt Engelbrektsson, Sweden's first great national hero. However, the struggle went on between those who were for and those who were against Swedish union with Denmark. Representatives from different groups of society gathered in Arboga in what is sometimes referred to as Sweden's first parliamentary meeting. Engelbrektsson was installed as head of government, but was murdered by the son of one of his enemies in 1436.

The turning point came in 1471, when Sten Sture led the Swedes in the Battle of Brunkeberg against the Danes. The Swedes won, but Denmark continued to exert control for another 50 years. Still, Swedish victory and Sture's subsequent role as statesman prevented Sweden from being completely absorbed into a union with Denmark.

Swedish nationalism led to further conflicts with the Danes, leading to the Bloodbath of Stockholm in 1520, when Denmark's King Christian II invaded Sweden, killed Sten Sture, and executed 82 leading noblemen. This terrible act eventually led to his downfall in the rebellion that followed. The leader of the rebellion, Swedish nobleman Gustav Vasa, whose father and other relatives were killed in the Bloodbath, was crowned king of Sweden in 1523.

GUSTAV VASA

Sometimes called "the George Washington of Sweden," King Gustav Vasa is credited with laying the foundations for Sweden's independence. The Swedes consider him the founder of their nation; June 6, the day he was crowned king in 1523, is today celebrated as Sweden's National Day.

During his reign, which lasted until 1560, Gustav Vasa made many important changes to the administration of the country. He made Stockholm the capital of Sweden and, to gain greater political control, seized the property of the Roman Catholic Church. He encouraged the spread of Protestantism and laid the ground for Lutheranism as Sweden's state religion.

In 1527 a national assembly with representatives of the four estates—nobles, clergymen, burghers, and peasants—was set up.

Following the German system, Gustav Vasa strengthened the power of the crown. In 1544 he declared a hereditary monarchy in Sweden. Previously, the king was elected, which meant that each time the throne was vacant, a lot of fighting took place among the Swedish nobility for power. In providing for a hereditary monarchy, Gustav Vasa became the founder of the Vasa dynasty that would rule Sweden for the next 300 years.

That same year, Gustav Vasa reformed the parliament and planned a form of national military service, making Sweden the first European country to have an army in peacetime.

This 17th-century warship, the Vasa, sank on its maiden voyage but was raised in 1961. It is now in the Vasa Museum of Stockholm.

SWEDISH EXPANSION

After Gustav Vasa's death, his sons struggled for the throne. From 1560 to 1611 the crown passed between three of his sons. But in spite of the infighting, Sweden prospered. The University of Uppsala, founded in 1477, flourished. Immigration was encouraged.

Sweden's next great king was Gustavus II Adolphus, grandson of Gustav Vasa. During his rule from 1611 to 1632, the kingdom expanded to include part of the Baltic states and Poland. Gustavus II also drove the Danes out of southern Sweden and made his country more powerful than Denmark for the first time.

Gustavus II was respected by many as a military genius. In 1632 he fought on the side of German Protestants against the Austrian Hapsburg empire in the Thirty Years War (1618–48). Swedish forces won the Battle of Lützen in 1632, but Gustavus II was killed in battle.

Gustavus II was succeeded by his daughter, Kristina, who was only 6 years old when she came to the throne. During her minority, the kingdom was governed by Axel Oxenstierna, who became the temporary regent. Sweden continued to expand its territories with more military conquests. Kristina converted from the Protestant faith to Roman Catholicism and abdicated in 1654.

Kristina's cousin, Karl X, maintained Sweden's expansionist policy. Under his reign, Sweden reached the height of its geographical size and political importance. It won Skåne province from Denmark, and after 1658, Sweden became a great power in northern Europe. The kingdom included Finland, provinces in northern Germany, and the Baltic state that is now known as Estonia. For a while, there was even a Swedish colony on the Delaware River in North America.

The next king, Karl XI, turned his attention homeward and gave his

Since Gustavus II Adolphus was away at war most of the time, his statesman Axel Oxenstierna administered Sweden and helped establish a new Supreme Court, reorganized the national assembly, extended the university at Uppsala, and fostered mining and other industries that contributed the bulk of the country's wealth.

people two decades of peace. He introduced several political reforms but also strengthened the position of the crown. He reduced the power of the nobility, who had gained strength during the wartime years when huge areas of land were given to them in exchange for supporting the monarchy. The nobles were made to surrender a large part of these lands to the crown and to the farmers.

But this peace did not continue. When Karl XII came to the throne at the end of the 17th century, Sweden became involved in wars again. During his rule from 1696 to 1718, Sweden lost much of its Baltic empire and parts of Finland to Russia. Karl XII's defeat in the 21-year Great Northern War against Denmark, Poland, and Russia reduced the country's borders to largely those of Sweden and Finland today.

The Royal Palace in Stockholm was rebuilt in 1760 after the earlier building was destroyed by fire in 1697. The original north wing still forms part of the present square-shaped palace, which encloses a courtyard and has two wings in the east and west.

ERA OF LIBERTY

Gustavus III was a popular king. He built hospitals, granted freedom of worship, and removed many state controls over the economy. Unfortunately, he was assassinated at a dance in the Stockholm Opera House by some members of the Swedish aristocracy, who were angry with him for siding with the commoners on too many issues.

In the 18th century, there was a struggle for power between the monarchy and the parliament. Tired of royal autocracy, the Swedish parliament introduced a new constitution after the death of Karl XII in 1718. This reduced the power of the monarchy.

Parliamentary government developed during the period from 1719 to 1772, called the Era of Liberty. The dominant party in parliament formed the government.

This era was dominated by two political groups: mercantile nobles called Hats and liberal commoners and urban traders called Caps. During this time, trade became increasingly important, and Sweden's economy prospered, although it remained dependent on agriculture. Swedish handmade goods soon found their way to Europe and beyond through trading organizations such as the Swedish East India Company. The government also encouraged iron and copper mining.

It was also an era of cultural and scientific growth. Parliament passed a Freedom of the Press Act in 1766, making Sweden one of the first countries in the world to protect press freedom. This act is still in force today. Many Swedes made important scientific contributions to the world: Carl von Linné, also called Linnaeus, created a system of classifying plants and animals that is used worldwide today; Anders Celsius invented the centigrade thermometer; Emmanuel Swedenborg made important discoveries in metallurgy, but is most well-known for his religious writings.

The final years of this period saw a power struggle in parliament between the nobility and the nonprivileged. King Gustavus III took advantage of the situation and reduced the power of the parliament through a bloodless coup in 1772. This marked the end of parliamentary rule and the reintroduction of absolute rule.

The narrow cobblestone streets of Gamla Stan, the oldest part of the city of Stockholm, bear testimony to the capital's medieval past.

Although the king's domestic policies were successful, Gustavus III is better remembered as a patron of the fine arts. During his rule, culture was encouraged and developed. He was responsible for the building of the Stockholm Dramatic Theater and the magnificent Royal Opera House. He also founded several academies for the fine arts, most notably the Swedish Academy of Literature, which is well known today for awarding the Nobel Prize for Literature.

In June 1905 King Oscar II opened the Swedish parliament, as Norway prepared to declare its independence.

NEW DYNASTY

During the Napoleonic Wars in the early 19th century, Sweden lost more of its territories—Finland to Russia and the German provinces to France—and faced an economic crisis. There was widespread unhappiness under the rule of Gustavus IV Adolphus, and he was deposed. His uncle, Karl XIII, was elected as the next king.

Parliamentary rule was again introduced. As Karl XIII had no heir, the parliament elected Jean-Baptiste Bernadotte, a French marshal close to Napoleon Bonaparte, to be heir to the throne in 1810. After the Napoleonic Wars in 1814, Bernadotte obtained large compensation for the loss of Sweden's Finnish lands and brought Norway under Swedish rule. His conservative policies won him the support of the old ruling class, but a liberal opposition began to form.

The reigns of his son and grandson, Oscar I and Karl XV, saw liberal ideas become reality. These included the setting up of compulsory education and elementary schools, the abolition of the guild system, and the implementation of free trade. Local self-government was introduced, and the parliament was restructured to follow a bicameral (two-chamber) system. This lasted until 1971, with the introduction of a unicameral parliament.

In the later half of the 19th century, rail transportation opened up forest industries. But Sweden remained poor, with 90 percent of its people dependent on agriculture. Many emigrated, mainly to North America, between 1866 and 1914. More than one million Swedes, or about one-fifth of the population, left for greener pastures.

THE 20TH CENTURY

The 20th century saw Sweden transformed into a modern industrial state. Universal suffrage was introduced for men in 1909 and for women in 1919. Sweden was among the first countries to give women the right to vote.

In 1905 Norway gained full independence from Sweden. Since the union with Norway in 1814, Sweden has not fought in any wars. During the two world wars, Sweden remained neutral. As a result, it was a safe haven for many refugees fleeing Nazi occupation in Europe.

One of the important events of the 20th century was the development of the welfare state. Its foundations were laid in the 1930s when the Social Democratic Party came to power. This party has dominated politics since 1932 and has held power for most of the last 70 years.

In September 1994, Sweden returned to a social democratic government, and even conservative political parties in Sweden accept most features of the welfare state. While no single party receives a majority of votes, the Social Democrats, being the country's largest party, govern in coalition with one or more smaller parties.

The *Riksdagshuset*, or Parliament House, in Stockholm is the seat of Sweden's parliament.

GOVERNMENT

SWEDEN IS a parliamentary democracy that also has a monarch. The constitution, consisting of three documents, contains the principles of government and provides the rights and freedoms of the people.

The most important document in the Swedish constitution is the Instrument of Government, which contains the basic rules of government and society. It states that all public power in Sweden comes from the people. It also states that democracy is based on "freedom of opinion and on universal and equal suffrage."

This document defines different types of rights and freedoms. Absolute rights, which cannot be restricted unless through a constitutional amendment, include freedom of worship, protection from being forced to declare political and religious views, protection of citizenship, and the prohibition of capital punishment. Rights that may be restricted by the law are freedom of speech, freedom of association, and protection from the restraint of liberty. The constitution also covers how far these restrictions may extend.

The second constitutional document is the Act of Succession, which regulates the succession to the throne. The third document, the Freedom of the Press Act, provides the right to publish without restrictions and allows citizens access to all public papers.

Above: **The changing of the Guard at the Royal Palace in Stockholm. The palace is the official residence and administrative office of the king and queen.**

Opposite: **The Parliament House in Stockholm.**

PARLIAMENT

Sweden's parliament, or *Riksdag* ("RICKS-dahg"), has 349 members. It is the main representative of the people. Members from different political parties are elected every four years. Swedes aged 18 and above have the right to vote, and voter turnout is usually high, at more than 80 percent, although voting is not compulsory.

Seats in parliament are allocated by a system of proportional representation; seats are distributed among the parties contesting the election in proportion to the number of votes they get. A qualification to this rule is that a party must win at least 4 percent of the national vote to get a seat.

The Swedish parliament has only one chamber. It is presided over by the speaker of parliament, who is responsible for proposing the prime minister for parliamentary approval.

The work of the parliament is carried out by 16 standing committees, each dealing with a different area, such as the constitution, finance and budgeting, and other concerns covered by the ministries. The job of the parliament is to approve national taxes, annual budgets, and legislation. The standing committees study bills proposed by the government and members of parliament and make their reports at a plenary session, which is when all members of parliament and the cabinet meet.

EXECUTIVE POWER

Political power lies with the cabinet and the party or parties to which ministers belong. The cabinet is made up of the prime minister and 21 ministers, who have to give up their right to vote in parliament if they join the cabinet; official substitutes take their places. Cabinet ministers are appointed by the prime minister. Sweden's current prime minister, who came to power in 1998, is Göran Persson.

THE MONARCHY

Sweden has a constitutional monarchy. The king is the head of state and performs official duties, such as opening the parliament every October. He has no political power and no role in politics. King Carl XVI Gustaf (*above, right*), a descendant of the Bernadotte family, came to the throne in 1973. He acts as the official representative of Sweden. His consort is Queen Silvia (*above, left*).

Carl XVI will be succeeded by his daughter, Crown Princess Victoria, who was born on July 14, 1977, the eldest of three children. The heir to the throne is the firstborn, and in 1979 the Act of Succession was amended to give men and women equal rights to the throne. The king and queen's two other children are Prince Carl Philip, born on May 13, 1979, and Princess Madeleine, born on June 10, 1982.

Sweden's royal family used to live in the Royal Palace. However, since 1981, they have lived in the Drottningholm Palace, a UNESCO World Heritage site, on the outskirts of the city.

Former Prime Minister Olof Palme. He was assassinated in 1986.

POLITICAL PARTIES

After World War I voting rights were expanded and political parties began to gain prominence. In the 1921 election, five parties were voted into parliament: the Social Democrats, the Communists, the Moderates, the Liberals, and the Centrists. The Social Democrats soon became the dominant party.

After the strikes and labor unrest of the 1920s and 1930s, the Social Democrats won the 1932 election and won every national election until 1976. This was the longest period of rule by Social Democrats anywhere in the world.

The socialist government introduced a mixed economy, where both the public and private sectors played important roles in economic development. Known as "the middle way," this form of government soon gained Sweden a reputation for industrial progress and political stability.

In the general election of 1976 the Social Democrats lost to a coalition of conservative parties. A Liberal Party minority government took over until 1982, when the Social Democrats won back a clear majority of votes. Olof Palme became the prime minister, but he was killed in 1986. Ingvar Carlsson, also from the Social Democrats, then became prime minister.

Since 1988, new political parties have formed, including the Environmental (Green) Party, the Christian Democratic Party, and the New Democracy Party. In 1991 the Swedes shifted their vote to the right. The Centrist, Moderate, Liberal, and Christian Democratic parties formed a coalition government, with Moderate Party leader Carl Bildt as prime minister. The conservative coalition governed until 1994.

RECENT ELECTIONS

Until recently, Swedish politics was a question of balancing two party blocks: the socialists (Social Democrats and ex-Communist Leftists) and the nonsocialists (Moderates, Liberals, Centrists, and Christians). In the election of 1994, voters rejected the nonsocialist-bloc incumbents and returned the Social Democrats to power. The Social Democrats won an even stronger majority in the 2002 election.

Despite economic woes from inflation and stagnation in the 1990s, Göran Persson's government has kept the welfare system rather than adopt a freer market (which would threaten the Swedish lifestyle). The Social Democrats have reduced Sweden's high tax rates and government spending and increased public sector employment, resulting in lower unemployment and inflation and a budget surplus in the new millenium.

Former Prime Minister Carl Bildt.

LOCAL GOVERNMENT

The Swedish administration is divided into 21 counties consisting of 288 municipalities in total. Each county is run by an elected council headed by a governor appointed at the federal level. Each municipality is also run by an elected council.

The county council is chiefly responsible for providing medical care and training nurses and other healthcare professionals. Besides a few government-run and private hospitals, the county councils own all hospitals in Sweden. County councils also see to the development of educational facilities, the proper functioning of social services, public transportation, industry, and tourism within the county.

Municipal councils have a lot of decision-making power in matters affecting residents within the municipality, such as child and elderly care, education in elementary, intermediate, and high school, taxes and service fees, garbage collection and disposal, and the supply of electricity and gas.

To fulfill their responsibilities, both county and municipal councils are entitled to levy taxes. They also receive federal subsidies.

THE OMBUDSMAN

The ombudsman is a Swedish concept, created to provide some kind of check on the work of public agencies. Besides monitoring these agencies, the ombudsman also looks into complaints from the public against unfair treatment. This idea has spread to other countries and institutions with the aim of protecting the individual.

The oldest form of ombudsmanship is the office of the parliamentary ombudsman that dates from 1809. It was created to give the parliament a safeguard for how laws were used by judges, civil servants, and military officers. Today there are four parliamentary ombudsmen who cover all national and municipal agencies in Sweden. These ombudsmen investigate thousands of complaints annually, choosing either to mediate or to take legal action against the offending party.

Other government-appointed ombudsmen include the competition ombudsman, whose job is to ensure fair business practices based on the law, and the consumer ombudsman, whose work is similar to Ralph Nader's in the United States. The consumer ombudsman tries to ensure that consumers are protected against misleading advertising, unsafe products, and improper business practices such as unreasonable contracts.

The press ombudsman is not appointed by the government but has been established by three national press organizations: the National Press Club, the Union of Journalists, and the Newspaper Publishers Association. The press ombudsman examines complaints by people who think that certain newspaper stories have violated press ethics and wish to be protected against the invasion of their privacy.

There are also ombudsmen who work against ethnic discrimination and unfair treatment based on sexual orientation, and ombudsmen who work for equality for the disabled.

The office of the equal opportunities ombudsman was set up in 1980 to ensure the observance of the law concerning sexual equality at work. Besides handling individual cases of discrimination in the workplace and in society, ombudsmen also help to shape public opinion and recommend ways to fight unequal treatment.

Swedes young and old wave the flag and cheer in a street procession.

A NEUTRAL COUNTRY

Sweden has adopted a policy of neutrality, which means that it does not align itself with any political or military alliance during peacetime and remains neutral in times of war.

Sweden has worked to become self-sufficient in agriculture, industry, and defense and is not a member of the North Atlantic Treaty Organization (NATO). In 1995, as a result of a countrywide referendum, Sweden joined the European Union, and in 2001 Prime Minister Persson served as the president of the Union.

Sweden joined the European Union only after it was able to guarantee its right to neutrality and get special permission to maintain higher-than-usual environmental regulations. Sweden has not yet joined the European Economic and Monetary Union, in which member countries adopted a single currency, the euro, in 2002.

THE SWEDISH FLAG

June 6, Sweden's National Day, was originally celebrated as Swedish Flag Day. This date was chosen because it was the day on which Gustav Vasa, founder of the Swedish state, was elected king in 1523. It was also on this day in 1809 that the country adopted a new constitution enshrining civil rights and liberties.

There are 15 official flag days in Sweden, including the special celebrations of the royal family, May Day, Election Day, and Nobel Day.

The design of Sweden's flag (*right*) follows that of Denmark's flag, while the colors—blue and yellow—are borrowed from the Swedish coat of arms. It is not known when the flag was first used.

THE NATIONAL COAT OF ARMS

Sweden has two national coats of arms: the Lesser and the Greater. The Lesser Coat of Arms is blue in color, with three crowns of gold and a closed crown sitting on top of a shield. This crown on top is sometimes encircled with the chain of the Order of the Seraphim, Sweden's most distinguished order. The triple crown design can be traced back to 1336 as the emblem of Sweden. It was then a symbol of the Three Wise Kings. The Lesser Coat of Arms is used more frequently than the Greater Coat of Arms, which belongs to the monarch.

The Greater Coat of Arms, the design of which dates back to the 15th century, is used only on special occasions by the government and parliament. The shield is divided into four parts and contains the triple crown and the "Folkung Lion," which was the arms of the ruling house from 1250 to 1364.

In the center are the arms of the present ruling house, the Bernadottes. These arms represent the Vasa dynasty, with the bridge representing the Italian principality of Ponte Corvo, a gift to Jean-Baptiste Bernadotte from Napoleon Bonaparte in 1809. The arms are complemented by the Napoleonic eagle and seven stars.

THE NATIONAL ANTHEM

Sweden's national anthem, *Du gamla, du fria* ("doo GAHM-lah, doo FREE-ah"), meaning "Thou ancient, thou freeborn," was written by a ballad writer, Richard Dybeck, in the 19th century. It was set to a folk melody from the province of Västmanland and was sung frequently at the turn of the century, before it became the national anthem.

ECONOMY

SWEDEN HAS A MIXED ECONOMY, in which private and state-owned enterprises exist side by side. This "Swedish model," a concept that came about in the late 1930s, refers to the way Sweden fostered prosperity by avoiding the pitfalls of both Communism and capitalism.

THE SWEDISH MODEL

Since 1932 Sweden's socialist government has steered "the middle way" by allowing the private and public sectors to develop together. This was very successful for many years. A key factor was the cooperation of the three main players in the economy: government, labor, and business. Unlike in other socialist nations, the government in Sweden did not nationalize key industries.

The public sector is one of the largest employers. It provides essential services, such as telecommunications and the postal service, and is responsible for education, health care, and social welfare. The other big employer is the business sector. Most businesses are privately owned, while the state and cooperative societies own a small proportion (about 10 percent).

The government has helped struggling industries like shipbuilding, steel, and forestry by taking a major ownership role. However, from 1991 until it was voted out, the conservative government tried to reduce the state's role in the economy. Although some state-owned industries were privatized, the government was not able to substantially decrease the role of the public sector in the economy because of the recession.

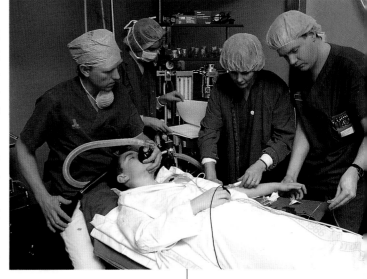

Above: **A patient undergoing surgery. Swedish healthcare is among the best in Europe.**

Opposite: **Göteborg harbor, first established in the 19th century, is today the largest harbor in the Nordic countries.**

MAJOR INDUSTRIAL SECTORS

Modern Swedish companies are characterized by specialized products, the use of high technology, and an emphasis on research and development. Industry is dominated by a few large companies, some of which are multinationals. More than 40 percent of the industrial labor force is employed by the country's 20 largest companies.

ENGINEERING is the largest sector of the economy, accounting for about 40 percent of industrial production and concentrated in southern and central Sweden, especially in the urban areas of Stockholm, Göteborg, and Malmö. This sector of the economy is highly dependent on trade; over half of its output is exported.

A Swedish airliner about to take to the skies. Swedish aircraft engineering is so advanced that the country has built its own jet fighters—like the *Saab Viggen*, one of the best in the world—to protect the country.

The engineering sector can be divided into four main subsectors: mechanical engineering, electrical engineering, the manufacture of transportation equipment, and metal fabrication. The most important subsector is the automotive industry, which exports 70 percent of its output. Two major manufacturers, Volvo and Saab-Scania, produce cars, trucks, buses, heavy engines, and aircraft components.

Electrical engineering and electronics form another vital sector where high technology is developed and used. Products include telecommunications systems, computers, and industrial robots. Telecommunications equipment accounts for 40 percent of electrical production. The ratio of robots to workers in Sweden is among the highest in the world.

CONSTRUCTION boomed in the 1960s and 1970s as a result of urban migration, increased demand for better housing, and easier financing for building projects. The domestic construction industry slowed down during the recession in the 1990s.

Internationally, Swedish construction companies have done well, helping to build infrastructural projects such as dams, harbors, railways, and power stations in many countries. The chief advantage of these companies lies in technical knowledge and project management. Their largest export markets are Middle Eastern and African countries.

Export construction projects are a vital factor in the long-term growth of Sweden's construction industry, which employs almost 20 percent of the total labor force.

Workers at the Volvo automobile plant outside Göteborg. Volvo is the second largest manufacturer of trucks in the world today.

Swedish economist Gunnar Myrdal once noted that Swedes have not only been lucky economically but have also made use of their luck. Their neutrality policy and leadership in UN peacekeeping activities have made them many friends. Through this, Sweden has developed close economic ties with many nations.

IRON AND STEEL provided the impetus for the industrialization thrust at the turn of the century. Today the production of engineered products flourishes as a result of the domestic manufacture of iron and nonferrous metal goods.

Although mining has now declined in importance, Sweden remains the largest iron ore exporter in Europe. About 90 percent of Sweden's iron comes from the great ore fields at Kiruna and Malmberget in the Lappland region. Copper, lead, zinc, silver, and gold are also mined in large amounts in the north.

Sweden is one of the world's biggest importers of steel. The domestic steel industry specializes in producing high-grade iron and steel for products such as ball bearings, razor blades, and watch and valve springs. About one-third of ordinary steel products are used in construction, shipbuilding, and other industries.

CHEMICALS were in production a hundred years ago in the form of fertilizers, explosives, and inorganic chemicals. Growth sectors today include organic chemicals, plastics, and pharmaceuticals. The chemical industry accounts for about 13 percent of industrial output.

The pharmaceutical industry, one of the biggest chemical subsectors, exports 80 to 90 percent of its output. Pharmaceuticals spends more money than any other industrial sector on research and development. Pharmaceutical research covers genetic engineering, drugs for heart disease, and eye surgery.

Biotechnology and its industrial uses, based mainly on knowledge from medical research, was a source of expansion in the 1980s. Swedish expertise in this area includes plant breeding, wastewater treatment, metal extraction, and processes for making plastics and other chemicals. More

recently, petrochemicals, a branch of organic chemistry, has been an engine of growth for the whole chemical industry.

Chemical production, usually part of an industrial group whose main interests are in metal production or the pulp industry, is mainly in the hands of some 50 companies. Usually of moderate size, these companies are found in a few industrial regions in the south and north, where pulp and paper mills provide by-products and a ready market.

One of Sweden's most well-known researchers in the chemical industry was Alfred Nobel, who lived in the 19th century. Nobel invented dynamite but is world-famous today for establishing the Nobel Prize, awarded each year to individuals who have excelled in their fields of work.

A Swedish icebreaker in port. Sweden's ship-building industry is concentrated in Göteborg.

FORESTRY

More than half of Sweden's land area is forested. The forestry industry is economically important to this country; it employs about 150,000 people and is the principal economic activity in many regions.

The forestry industry produces paper, paperboard, pulp, sawn timber, and other wood products. It is dominated by large companies with their

A forklift hauling wood for export. One-quarter of Sweden's forests are owned by the state; the rest are privately owned.

own forests, transportation facilities, and manufacturing plants. The Swedish lumber industry is the largest in Western Europe, producing about 3.5 percent of the world output. Sweden's wood is exported mostly to Great Britain, Germany, Denmark, and the Netherlands.

AGRICULTURE

Only 7 percent of Sweden's land is cultivated for agriculture. Most of the farms and cultivated land are privately owned, and work is carried out mainly by families. Less than 3 percent of the labor force is engaged in agriculture. Although resources devoted to agriculture are small, it is nevertheless a vital activity. Swedish farmers use improved irrigation methods, fertilizers, and high-yield seeds to get the best agricultural output. In the warmer south, crops include wheat, sugar beets, potatoes, oil seeds, and peas. In central Sweden, cereals, fodder grain, and plants that yield oil are cultivated. In the colder north, where the growing season is shorter, animal fodder, vegetables, and seed potatoes are grown.

The fertile plains in the southern county of Skåne produce a large portion of the country's food supplies. Skåne is sometimes called "the granary of Sweden."

A petroleum terminal in Stockholm.

FOREIGN TRADE

Sweden depends heavily on trade. It exports a great deal of its produce and also imports goods to meet domestic demand. Exports of goods and services account for around 30 percent of the gross domestic product.

The main export goods are machinery, motor vehicles, paper products, pulp and wood, chemicals, as well as iron and steel products. Also on the increase is the export of healthcare systems.

Imports largely consist of industrial input goods, either finished in Sweden or used as components. Major imports include motor vehicles, petroleum and petroleum products, machinery, foodstuff, raw materials, chemical products, iron and steel, and consumer and investment goods.

Over half of Sweden's trade is with other European nations: Germany, Great Britain, Norway, Denmark, France, and Finland. The United States is Sweden's third largest customer and fourth largest supplier. Exports to the United States include paper and paperboard, scientific instruments, consumer goods, and automobiles.

TRADE UNIONS

Sweden is known for its relatively stable labor force. More than 50 percent of the population works, and more than three-quarters of all eligible employees are union members.

Sweden has three national union confederations. The Swedish Trade Union Conference (LO), for blue-collar unions, brings together more than 90 percent of workers. The Central Organization of Salaried Employees covers 75 percent of white-collar employees, and the Confederation of Professional Associations is also for white-collar workers.

Sweden had a system of centralized wage bargaining until a framework on wages and working conditions was worked out between the LO and the main employers' federation. Today negotiations on such matters take place only at the level of the individual industry.

A fisherman cleans a fish while his customer looks on. Pollution in the Baltic Sea is seriously affecting the fishing industry in Sweden.

ENVIRONMENT

SWEDEN IS A "GREEN" COUNTRY, with a long-term commitment to cleaning up the environment and maintaining natural diversity for future generations. Manufacturing and farming have taken their toll on the environment, and both the government and the people are working to try to undo some of the damage already done and minimize further damage.

THE FORESTS

Sweden is blessed with extensive forest cover: pine and coniferous forests in the northern region and deciduous forests of oak, elm, ash, hazelnut, and beech in the southern region. Some of Sweden's many wild plants and flowers, such as poppies, pasque flowers, and orchids, are protected by law.

Above: **King's Garden is a beautiful park that is popular with Swedes living in Stockholm.**

Opposite: **The coasts of Sweden are relatively clean, thanks to its environmentally conscious people.**

Many animals make their home in these forests. The king of Swedish wildlife is the moose. This majestic mammal, related to the great North American moose, stands more than 6 feet (2 m) tall. Moose are abundant in most of Sweden except in the far north.

Smaller inhabitants of Sweden's forests include roe and fallow deer. Most of the country's predators are not as abundant as its population of deer. Wolves number only about 100; wolverines also total around 100. Their numbers are linked, as wolverines depend on wolf droppings to survive. Both animals are protected by law.

Sweden's most common predator is the red fox, and its largest is the brown bear, weighing up to 772 pounds (350 kg). The lynx is Sweden's only wild cat. There are only about 1,000 lynx and 1,000 brown bears living wild in the remote areas of the country. Some counties allow limited hunting of lynx and brown bears.

AIRBORNE AND AQUATIC TREASURES

With the longest coastline in Europe at 4,536 miles (7,300 km) and thousands of inland lakes, Sweden is home to numerous fish and birds. Nevertheless, birds of prey such as eagles and hawks are limited in numbers. Hunting them is prohibited, and efforts are being made to protect the wetlands, so critical to the survival of many bird species.

The inland lakes support large populations of salmon, capable of growing to more than 38 pounds (17 kg) in weight. Salmon fishing has a long tradition in Sweden. Anglers need a licence to fish for salmon.

About 6,000 seals live in Sweden's Baltic waters. Sweden works with its neighbors to protect the Baltic gray seal from poachers who hunt it for its fur. Gray seals give birth in the winter or autumn, and the pups are a target for poachers because of their fluffy white coat.

Right: **A newborn gray seal pup on an ice floe. It can grow up to 9.8 feet (3 m) in length and 660 pounds (300 kg) in weight.**

Opposite: **Pollution monitors in central Stockholm.**

ENVIRONMENTAL CONCERNS

Environmental problems in Sweden come from industrial, agricultural, and consumer waste. From years of fertilizing farmland, Sweden's rivers and lakes contain large quantities of nitrogen and phosphorous washed into the water system by run-off. This abundance of nutrients has resulted in the rapid growth of algae, which depletes the shallow waters of oxygen in the summer. This phenomenon, called eutrophication, also affects the nearby Baltic Sea.

Heavy industries often release sulphur dioxide into the air; when mixed with rainwater, sulphur dioxide turns into acid rain, which burns plants and makes water systems unfit for fish and animal life. It is difficult to control sulphur dioxide emissions as they do not stay within national boundaries; emissions from northern Europe and southern Sweden combine to damage Sweden's northern lakes and forests.

Another environmental concern in Sweden is global warming from the emission of greenhouse gases produced from burning fossil fuels such as oil and gas. Sweden has also banned the use of chlorofluorocarbons (CFCs) as aerosol propellants to try to prevent further destruction of the Earth's ozone layer.

RESOLUTE PROTECTORS

Swedish love and respect for nature materialized into serious efforts to protect the environment in the 1970s, when the Swedes realized that the country's beautiful forests and lakes were being destroyed by heavy industry. Sweden has become a leader in implementing environmental laws and controls. One of the country's main concerns when debating whether to join the European Union was whether it would be able to continue its environmental reforms. Sweden was concerned that other members of the Union might resist the high standards of environmental protection Sweden wished to maintain.

Greenpeace activists try to block the path of a ship carrying 3,500 tons of waste from the Netherlands before it docks at a port south of Stockholm.

ECONOMIC METHODS

Sweden is a case study in environmental regulation that proves that economic methods can work well. For example, making companies with high sulphur emissions pay a higher tax than companies with reduced emissions brought emissions down by around 80 percent between 1980 and 1996. A tax on nitrogen oxide, a by-product of incineration plants, also reduced emissions by 80 percent from pre-tax levels.

Farmers are not exempted; they must pay a tax for the use of chemical fertilizers and pesticides. These taxes have funded projects to help clean up farm waste.

Municipalities charge a waste disposal tax to encourage people to reduce the amount of garbage they produce. Manufacturers are legally responsible for collecting and recycling drink bottles, tires, and some forms of packaging. These methods have helped Sweden generate less pollution and keep the use of harmful substances at lower than normal levels for an industrial country.

Recycling bins are common in Stockholm.

Dancers at a recycling festival.

A NEW LAW

In 1998 the Environmental Code was enacted by the parliament. This powerful legislation replaces 15 other environmental laws, which were often confusing and contradictory, with a single national plan and set of regulations. The goal of the code is to achieve ecological sustainability within one generation, that is, by 2020 to 2025. This is an ambitious goal that will require many changes in industry, farming, and everyday living. The hope is that the Environment Code will create a sustainable economy and lifestyle for the Swedes.

INTERNATIONAL COOPERATION

Swedes are also active in supporting and promoting international accords and agreements to protect the global environment. For example, Sweden and the European Union have signed the Kyoto Protocol, an international agreement binding members to reduce greenhouse gas emissions by 8 percent below 1990 levels by 2008 to 2012.

Under the Kyoto Protocol, each country is given a target for reduction, or if they already produce less than normal, they may increase emissions. Sweden is allowed to increase its emissions by 4 percent but has decided to further reduce emissions by another 2 percent in the same time period. While most countries who signed the Kyoto Protocol are worried about not being able to meet their targets, Sweden is going beyond the call of duty to try to help save the world from the worsening effects of global warming.

THE RIGHT OF COMMON ACCESS

The Swedes believe in the right of the individual to enjoy the beauty of nature. They have a common agreement: all open and natural spaces should be accessible to all people at all times. This right dates back centuries and is not legal but moral. Swedes know and understand this rule and do not need to be told by law or the government how it works. Tour guides are required to explain the right of common access to non-Swedish visitors. This right means that the natural environment is everyone's concern, no matter where they live or what they do.

ACCESS The right of common access gives people permission to do certain things on all open, noncultivated land and private roads: walk, cycle, ride a horse, or ski; pick nonprotected wild flowers, berries, mushrooms, fallen pine cones, acorns, and beechnuts; camp or park a trailer for 24 hours; let their pets run free; make a campfire; and bathe or boat on open water courses and use the water to drink.

RESPONSIBILITY The right of common access also demands that everyone act responsibly and follow certain guidelines. People are expected not to damage or pollute the land or water; not to enter farms, plantations, or private gardens near people's homes; not to use a motorized vehicle on private lands unless the owner gives permission; not to pick flowers or uproot plants that are protected by law; not to let their pets run free in private hunting lands; and not to make a fire where or when it may cause damage.

A NATURE-LOVING WORLD

Sweden is a global leader when it comes to environmental protection, because, in general, they "practice what they preach." Swedes want the world's future generations to enjoy a safe, clean, and beautiful natural environment. They are prepared to lead the way in adopting tough measures to change bad habits and enforcing tough penalties for those who resist. From the Environment Code to the right of common access, Sweden is setting the standard for the rest of world, hoping to spread their love and respect for nature and remind people everywhere of their role as protector of nature.

SWEDES

MOST SWEDES ARE DESCENDED from Germanic tribes that came to Scandinavia thousands of years ago. While many Swedes are tall, blonde, and blue-eyed, since the arrival of migrants from many parts of the world in the 1940s, Sweden has had a more ethnically diverse population. Today, about 1 million Swedes are either immigrants themselves or have an immigrant parent.

DEMOGRAPHY

The first complete population census, taken in 1749, counted 1.8 million people. The number rose to 3.5 million in 1850 and 7 million in 1950. Today, Sweden's population stands at 8.9 million.

Sweden's population is very unevenly distributed. Most Swedes live in the southern part of the country. Stockholm's population density, for example, is 749 people per square mile (281 people per square km), compared to only 8 people per square mile (3 people per square km) in Norrbotten, one of the northernmost counties in Norrland. The national average is 52 people per square mile (19.7 per square km).

Over 80 percent of the population lives in urban communities, with the cities being the main centers of population. Most of the population growth that took place between 1950 and 1970 occurred in three main areas: around Stockholm and Lake Mälaren, on the western coast around Göteborg; and around Malmö in the south. Today, almost half of the Swedish population lives in these areas.

Above: **Swedish students celebrate graduation day.**

Opposite: **A modern Swede.**

PAST POPULATION MOVEMENTS

Between the 1850s and 1930, Sweden experienced a wave of mass emigration. A growing population, the lack of work, and poverty created social problems. Harvest failures and famine between 1853 and 1873 drove about 103,000 people, or 3 percent of the population, to the United States, especially Minnesota, Nebraska, and Wisconsin.

Between 1879 and 1893, after an economic slump in Sweden and a boom in the United States, about 34,000 Swedes emigrated each year to North America.

By 1900 the Swedish economy had fallen below that of Norway. About 1.5 million people left Sweden between the 1850s and 1930. Some 80 percent of these went to North America, the rest to other Nordic countries. Many stayed for good in their new

The Swedish population reflects an ethnic diversity produced by decades of mass migrations.

homeland, while about one-quarter of the emigrants eventually returned.

Post-World War II industrial expansion created a great demand for immigrant labor, and Swedish companies actively recruited from other European countries. In the 1950s the Nordic countries set up a common labor market, allowing citizens of one Nordic country to work or study in another. In 1967 Sweden introduced immigration controls, leading to a drop in the number of immigrants.

POPULATION TRENDS

Sweden has an aging population. With quality healthcare and high living standards, older people are living longer. Sweden now has a life expectancy of 82 years for women and 77 years for men. In the past 40 years, the proportion of people over 64 years old has doubled.

Nevertheless, Sweden also has a good proportion of young people. Children under the age of 14 account for 18 percent of the population. Sweden has a birth rate of 9.91 babies born per 1000 population, one of the highest in Europe. This is partly because Swedish women born in the 1950s and 1960s have delayed having children until they are 30 or 40 years old, owing to their increased involvement in the labor force. However, the number of births is expected to decline, as these women pass childbearing age and the number of younger women in Sweden gradually falls.

Children having fun at an amusement park.

A Sami family welcomes Santa Claus and his reindeer.

THE SAMI

The Sami are a minority people who live in arctic Sweden. It is believed that the Sami came in nomadic groups from central Russia during pre-Christian times, travelling through southern Finland and settling in northern Scandinavia.

Today, 50,000 to 60,000 Sami are found all over the entire Finnish-Scandinavian arctic region and along the mountains on both sides of the Swedish-Norwegian border. About 17,000 Sami live in Sweden and vary in their commitment to their culture. Some Sami identify themselves strongly as a separate ethnic group, while others have been assimilated into Swedish culture.

The Samis' traditional occupation was breeding reindeer. However, today, only some 3,000 Sami still breed reindeer for meat and milk. The importance of reindeer breeding can be seen in the way breeders belong to a village, which serves not just as a grazing area but also an administrative unit. Common facilities are built and maintained by the village, and the cost is shared among the residents.

Over the years, the Sami have given up their nomadic lifestyle for permanent settlements in the low fell region, where mountain reindeer mate and reproduce. However, reindeer breeding is not very profitable, as a herd of at least 500 is needed to earn enough money for the family. Also, the 1986 nuclear accident at Chernobyl in the former Soviet Union has had a lasting impact on the reindeer, and it will be many years before reindeer meat will be fit for consumption again.

Many Sami families supplement their income by hunting, fishing, selling handicrafts, and hosting tourists. Sami handicrafts made from traditional materials can be found at the winter market fair in Jokkmokk. The Samis' traditional food is reindeer meat and milk and cheese made from reindeer milk. One delicacy is *lappkok* ("LAHP-shehk"), a broth of reindeer marrow bones and shredded liver.

The Sami language belongs to the Finno-Ugric group and has three dialects. The most widely used is North Sami, spoken in northern Sweden, Norway, and the far north of Finland. South Sami is spoken in north-central Sweden and central Norway. East Sami is spoken in eastern Finland and the Kola Peninsula in Russia.

Sami children go to a regular state-supported school or a state-run nomad school. Both have the same aims, except that the nomad school includes the teaching of Sami language and culture. Children in regular schools learn their language and culture at home through a special home language project.

Without a strong written tradition, Sami culture has been passed down orally in a form of singing called *jojking* ("YOI-king").

Today, Sami reindeer herders may use snow scooters, motor vehicles, or even aircraft to follow their herds.

A group of men contemplate a game of giant chess. Sweden's population includes immigrants from other European countries and the Middle East.

FINNS

Sweden also has a Finn minority in the far north, in the Lappland region and the county of Norrbotten. Most Swedish Finns live near the border with Finland.

Swedish Finns number around 30,000. On a daily basis, they speak Finnish, although they can also speak Swedish, which they learned in school. Many of their customs and traditions are closer to Finnish than Swedish culture. Some Finns are recent migrants; others have been in Sweden for generations.

SWEDEN'S CHANGING FACE

Immigrants accounted for more than 40 percent of Sweden's population growth between 1944 and 1980. Since World War II immigrants have played an increasingly important role in Sweden.

Being a neutral country during the war, Sweden welcomed refugees from other Nordic and Baltic states. Many returned home after the war, but some remained as there was a demand for labor.

Many immigrants also came from Finland, Norway, and Denmark when an agreement was signed in 1954 creating a common labor market among these countries.

A Swedish mother and child. Until the mid-20th century, Sweden was almost ethnically homogeneous. Immigration has since created a nation of greater ethnic diversity.

In the 1960s Sweden experienced two big waves of immigration due to growing industrialization. The first wave, in the mid-1960s, saw the arrival of workers from former Yugoslavia, Greece, Italy, Germany, Turkey, and Poland. The second wave took place between 1968 and 1970, with most immigrants coming from Finland.

As the economy slowed down in the 1970s, so did the inflow of foreign workers. The government also took steps to restrict immigration.

Today, most immigrants are political refugees from Slovenia, Romania, Chile, Iran, Iraq, Somalia, and Ethiopia. The government has introduced measures to help integrate newcomers into Swedish society. These aim to establish equality between immigrants and Swedes, freedom of cultural choice and cooperation, and solidarity between the Swedish majority and the various ethnic minorities.

INTEGRATING IMMIGRANTS

Some 30 national immigration organizations have been set up through government grants to give minority groups a collective voice. There are newspapers printed in 12 different languages to keep the immigrant population informed of events in Sweden.

Language programs for newly arrived adults include courses in Swedish and are paid for by the government. There are also home language programs for immigrant children to learn their native language to help preserve Sweden's ethnic cultures.

Also significant is the right of foreigners who have lived in Sweden for at least three years to vote and run for office in local and regional elections. Non-citizens have the same rights as Swedes with regard to social benefits and education.

FOLK DRESS

More than 400 types of folk clothing are worn in Sweden. Originally peasant wear, these are now worn on festive occasions or as formal attire, no longer for the same functions or with the same significance as before.

Each traditional outfit is recognizable through the type of fabric used, the embroidery, and the accessories, among other things. Not all folk outfits today are exact replicas of those worn in past centuries; many have been redesigned with a modern twist.

There are many elements to the complete folk outfit, and there are strict rules for wearing it correctly. A woman's traditional outfit usually consists of a white cotton or linen blouse with long, sometimes puffy, sleeves; a skirt, embroidered at the hem and gathered at the waist; a vest,

apron, shawl, and bonnet or hat; a purse; silver jewelry; and stockings and shoes.

In the 19th century Gustaf Ankarcrona and Carl Larsson designed a national folk dress for women that included a blue skirt with a yellow apron, and a red bodice embroidered with white daisies.

A man's traditional outfit consists of a long-sleeved white cotton shirt, a vest, knee-length trousers, and knee-high stockings. A rimmed hat and a knee-length embroidered coat may top off the outfit. A hat band or braid indicates whether the man is married or single.

Unmarried girls in some regions braid their hair and bind it with a red band or wear an open-ended bonnet, while in other regions, they do not cover their hair. Married women traditionally keep their heads covered all the time, with a white linen bonnet or a stiff frame cap. The headgear indicates whether the woman is going to a festive occasion or a sad one.

LIFESTYLE

SWEDES ARE GENERALLY quiet and reserved. It is in their character to be *snäll* ("snell"), meaning pleasant and considerate, especially toward elders. Family ties are very important in Swedish society, although the extended family model is disappearing, as the welfare state reduces couples' financial dependence on their relatives. Limited housing in the cities is an added reason for smaller families.

Swedes are also a hardworking people. Many believe that hard work is essential to support a welfare state.

Below: **Children on an excursion on the island of Ulvön, Ångermanland.**

Opposite: **Swedish children enjoy a midsummer celebration.**

THE STATE PROVIDES

The way of life for the average Swede is to a large extent defined by the welfare state, which provides basic social, educational, and medical services ranging from the district doctor to daily child-care. Users of these services pay a small fee according to how much they earn.

To finance the welfare state, Swedes pay some of the highest income taxes in the world. These high taxes have been a heavy burden, and in the 1991 election, many Swedes shifted their support away from the socialist party that shaped the welfare system. Nevertheless, the Swedish people put the Social Democrats back in power in 1994, and the welfare system continued, although efforts began to reduce tax rates.

*Opposite: **A proud mother with her baby.***

EDUCATION

Every Swedish child has access to formal education, regardless of his or her parents' income. There are a few private schools, but the majority of children attend state-run schools. All Swedish children are required to complete 12 years of compulsory education.

Most children start school at age 7, but they can start at age 6 if their parents prefer. Children spend nine years in *grundskola* ("GROOND-skol -lah"), a comprehensive school program divided into three stages: lower school (grades 1 to 3), middle school (grades 4 to 6), and upper school (grades 7 to 9). Grades 1 to 6 are the equivalent of elementary and junior high school in the United States. All children learn the same subjects in grades 1 to 6, with English introduced in grade 3. When they reach grade 7, they can choose the courses they want to study.

After grade 9, children must attend three years at *gymnasium* ("gim-NAH-sium"), or senior high school. At the end of *gymnasium*, students celebrate with a big graduation party. About one-third of young Swedes go on to study at one of Sweden's more than 40 colleges and universities. Students are entitled to apply for a state loan to pay college fees, and this is repaid after graduation, upon getting a job.

CARING FOR CHILDREN

For most Swedes with children, the day begins with dropping the children off at a childcare center or at school before going to work. About 60 percent of preschool children attend a *daghem* ("DAHG-hem"), or day-care center. When they start school, they still go to the day-care center after school is over and wait for their parents to pick them up after work.

Sweden's well-developed system of child-care centers has allowed Swedish women to work outside the home. At the same time, the high cost of living and high taxes mean that both partners must work so that the family can live comfortably.

The welfare state offers several benefits to the people so that they can combine work with having a family. When a young couple have a child, they make use of generous paid leave offered in no other country. Under Swedish law, a parent is entitled to 450 days of paid leave after the birth of the child—at 80 percent of the regular wage in the first 360 days and a smaller fixed sum in the next 90 days. Sometimes this leave is shared between the mother and father. Although fathers have not made use of this benefit as much as mothers, it is quite common to see men pushing strollers in the mall in the middle of a working day. This leave can also be delayed and spread over eight years.

Swedes love children, and they have taken great pains to ensure that children's rights are protected. Swedish children have their own ombudsman to look after their interests. The child ombudsman reports cases of abuse of minors to the social welfare committee, which investigates and intervenes where necessary.

SOCIAL INTERACTION

Climate influences social relationships in this cold, northern country. The pattern of work and play is related to the short, bitterly cold winter days and the long, warm summer days. This is especially true the farther north one goes.

In the past, when winter set in, many Swedes kept to a routine of working and going home. As temperatures fell, the streets of cities and towns quickly emptied by 7 P.M. The country seemed quieter, and there is less social interaction outside of the office and family. Christmas appeared to be the only time they had fun during the long, dark winter.

Today, however, winter provides the opportunity for Swedes to participate in sports such as skiing. Sweden is home to over 400 ski lodges

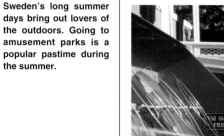

Sweden's long summer days bring out lovers of the outdoors. Going to amusement parks is a popular pastime during the summer.

and resorts. Playgrounds and parks that adjoin apartment complexes are also extensive and well-lit, and are enjoyable playgrounds for children.

As spring arrives and the days grow longer, another transformation occurs in the Swedish disposition. As the snow and ice melt, the people also seem to thaw, warmed by the sunshine. They shed their moody expressions, becoming more cheerful and patient. Social interaction becomes more spirited; the casual short greetings of winter turn into laughter and lively conversation. Outdoor cafés spring to life, filled with people socializing and making up for the inactive winter.

During the warmer months, people engage in a variety of outdoor activities. Families and friends, now seemingly less stressed, organize summer barbecues and picnics and make summer vacation plans. The most important summer event is the midsummer festival, held on the longest day of the year.

Relaxing by the sea and having a drink—the best way to spend a lazy summer day.

EQUALITY FOR WOMEN

Sweden is a society with few class differences. It is difficult to notice any distinction between the working class and the middle class. In the 1960s fast economic growth brought about a uniformly high standard of living, distributing income around the country. Today, the income gap between skilled and unskilled workers is relatively narrow, and the tax system further closes this gap.

Ulrika Hydman, one of Sweden's leading glass designers.

Attention is now focused on establishing equality between men and women. The government has tried to help both men and women to attain economic independence. Steps have been taken to make it easier for women to hold a job as well as have a family. Women make up half the Swedish labor force, and it is rare for someone to be without a job, whether part-time or full-time, even if they have children.

It is not surprising that Sweden has the highest rate of working women in Europe. The state encourages young mothers to continue working by granting long periods of paid leave to either parent when a child is born and by funding quality care facilities for children once they reach their first birthday. Most women go back to work after their maternity leave.

However, many occupations pay women less than they pay men, although the wage differential is small compared with other countries. Steps have been taken to give women more choices, but they continue to bear more responsibility than do men in taking care of the children and the domestic chores.

INDEPENDENT ELDERLY

The extended family has largely lost its importance in Sweden, because many people have moved from their hometowns to work in other parts of the country. As a result, many elderly may enjoy family visits only on weekends, if the family lives close by, or less frequently, although contact is maintained through other means.

The elderly are often cared for by the state rather than by their relatives. Retirees are given pensions and housing allowances that ensure financial security and some degree of independence.

Above: **Occupants of service apartments have nurses to care for them.**

p76: **A young mother and her kids. On average, Swedish women marry at age 23.**

p77: **A family of six equipped for a day out.**

More than 90 percent of Swedes age 65 and above live in ordinary homes, some modified to meet their needs. Without a younger relative living with them, many elderly use home-help services for their daily chores, such as shopping, cleaning, and cooking. District doctors and nurses make home calls to treat ill or housebound elderly. At the same time, municipalities run centers where the elderly get the opportunity to meet others and socialize.

Old people who are fairly fit can choose to live in service houses, apartment buildings that are owned and managed by the municipality. Residents at service houses enjoy subsidized home help and facilities such as a restaurant and activity rooms. Those who are less able to care for themselves live in old-age homes where 24-hour care is provided. Such homes, however, are being phased out as more state support is given for the elderly in their own residences.

MARRIAGE AND COHABITATION

Cohabitation, or living together without being married, is a common living arrangement in Sweden. The Swedish word for living together is *samboende* ("SAHM-BOH-ehn-deh"), which refers to the person one is living with. Many unmarried couples who live together have children; there are also single-parent families.

During the 1970s and 1980s the number of marriages fell as the number of cohabiting couples rose. In 1987 half of all babies in Sweden were born to single or cohabiting mothers. In the 1990s marriage seemed to come back in style, as more people rediscovered traditional family values.

Nevertheless, Sweden has one of the lowest marriage rates in the industrialized world. One couple in five lives together—five times the number in the United States. At the same time, many married couples in Sweden eventually separate. The country has one of the highest divorce rates in Europe; about 50 percent of Swedish marriages end in divorce.

Many couples in Sweden choose to live together as a temporary measure, postponing marriage until both partners are more settled in their jobs. Often, children attend their parents' wedding.

RURAL LIFESTYLE

A few generations ago, most of Sweden's population was rural. Industrialization in the 20th century pulled many Swedes away from their farms and villages and to the cities.

Today, more than 80 percent of Sweden's population live in cities, although Swedes still like the country life. Many city people own vacation homes in the country where they can take a break from the rush of the city to enjoy the country life.

NAMES

Swedish names can sound so similar that sometimes it is difficult to distinguish them. Until a century ago, many Swedish families did not have surnames. A person had a given name and a father's first name. Peter, whose father's name was John, was "Peter John's son," or Peter Johnson. His sister Greta was Greta Johndotter. Their father might have been "John Carl's son," or John Carlson.

Today, everyone has a first and a family name. But since many surnames end in "-son," the phone book might list hundreds of John Carlsons. So phone books specify the person's occupation to distinguish John Carlson the teacher from John Carlson the engineer.

RELIGION

CHRISTIANITY CAME TO SWEDEN in A.D. 829 when a French Benedictine monk called Ansgar arrived at Birka to spread the gospel. But it was not until the 11th century, when systematic evangelization took place, that the country became Christianized. The town of Uppsala was made the seat of the archbishop in 1164, and the first Swedish archbishop was eventually appointed.

Early Christianity in Sweden was of the Roman Catholic faith. After breaking up with Norway and Denmark, Gustav Vasa reduced the economic power of the Roman Catholic Church in Sweden. In 1527 he started the Protestant Reformation at Västerås. Olavus Petri, an Örebro native who had been inspired by Martin Luther and other European reformers, and his brother, Laurentius Andreae, the king's chancellor, were the driving force behind the Reformation in Sweden.

Left: **A 17th-century chapel with painted walls.**

Opposite: **The Great Church, built in the 13th century.**

THE REFORMATION

Olavus Petri contributed to Swedish Protestantism in many ways. He prepared a hymnbook, a church manual, and liturgy for the people and helped translate the Bible into Swedish.

In 1544 Sweden became a Protestant country when it was officially proclaimed a Lutheran kingdom. The king became head of the Church of Sweden. Some Roman Catholic priests left Sweden rather than accept Protestantism; others stayed and, together with the people, gradually accepted Protestantism. The Roman Catholic Church later attempted to regain power but failed.

Lutheranism became more firmly established in Sweden during the reign of Gustavus II Adolphus (1611–32). In the 18th and 19th centuries, however, the Pietism revival movement swept the Lutheran Church, as people turned to home bible sharing and prayer and fellowship in small groups for a deeper, more personal religious experience.

As a result of Pietism, education, social welfare, and mission activities were carried out by Christians in Sweden. The Church of Sweden has been active in promoting the unity and cooperation of Christians around the world.

LUTHERANISM

The origins of the Lutheran Church go back to Martin Luther, the 16th-century Roman Catholic priest who objected to some Catholic practices and started a movement known as the Protestant Reformation. Through his actions and writings, he ushered in not only Protestantism, but also a seedbed for new economic, political, and social thought.

Like all Christians, Lutherans believe in the divinity and humanity of Jesus Christ and in the Trinity of God. They also have two sacraments: baptism and the Lord's Supper. The basic unit of government in the Lutheran Church is the congregation. It is led by either a pastor or a lay person elected from the membership of a council, which is made up of a congregation's clergy and elected lay persons.

THE CHURCH OF SWEDEN TODAY

The Lutheran Church of Sweden is still the dominant faith in the country and is professed by 87 percent of the population. This is partly because when Swedish children are born they automatically become members of the Church if at least one parent is a member. However, the parents can renounce the child's membership within six weeks of birth. Members can also leave the church at any time.

Despite its large church membership, Sweden is basically a secular state, and religion plays a minor role in the lives of most Swedes. Only a small minority of the population attend church regularly, and church attendance tends to be greater in areas where various revival movements took place in the 19th century. Christian customs also vary greatly in different parts of the country.

Swedes generally keep Christian customs by marrying in church, getting their children baptized and confirmed, and holding church funeral services. More than 70 percent of babies are baptized and 90 percent of funerals performed by the Church of Sweden.

Until 1991 the Church of Sweden was responsible for maintaining population records, which it had done since the 17th century. Until the latter half of the 18th century, all Swedes were expected to be a part of the Church of Sweden. In 1781, the Edict of Toleration was issued, allowing other religious groups to practice their faith in the country. Full religious freedom was guaranteed by law only in 1952.

Unlike in some other Christian churches, the Church of Sweden has been ordaining women ministers since 1958.

A young woman wears the traditional headdress of candles in celebration of Saint Lucia Day.

Opposite: **A church in Uppsala, the town that holds the seat of the arch-bishop of the Church of Sweden.**

OTHER CHURCHES

The Roman Catholic Church has the second largest congregation in Sweden, especially after a recent boost to its membership generated by immigration from Catholic countries.

There are a few Protestant denominations in Sweden besides the Lutheran Church. Known as the "free churches," these include the Pentecostal movement, which gained prominence in the early 20th century in the United States and has since spread rapidly to other parts of the world.

Pentecostal services are enthusiastic and rousing, with an emphasis on music and lively congregational participation. Pentecostal churches are attractive to people who are interested in social reforms and an alternative to the orthodoxy of the Church of Sweden.

The second largest Protestant denomination in Sweden, Pentecostal churches are still growing in membership, the fastest growing religious movement in the country.

Another growing Protestant denomination is the Mission Covenant Church of Sweden. Some of Sweden's Protestant churches were founded as a reaction to the perceived rigidity of the Church of Sweden, while others were imported from other countries.

OTHER RELIGIONS

Close to half a million Muslims form the largest group of non-Christians in Sweden. Swedish Muslims are mainly immigrants from Turkey, the Middle East, and North Africa.

Sweden's third largest religious group are the Jews, who have had congregations in Sweden for over two centuries. There are also small numbers of Buddhists, Hindus, and Jehovah's Witnesses.

LANGUAGE

THE SWEDISH LANGUAGE comes from the North Germanic family of languages and is closely related to the Danish, Norwegian, Icelandic, and Faeroese languages. Modern Swedish, *Svenska* ("svenska"), developed from primitive Norse, the language of the Vikings.

The earliest language source in Sweden can be traced to runic inscriptions. The most common material for runes was wood, none of which have been preserved. Runes have also been found on stone, weapons such as spears and blades, and ornaments such as brooches.

RUNESTONES

The earliest runestones are from the eighth century. Little is known about their origin, but they were thought to be linked to magic and sorcery. From these stones we have learned about the political, economic, and cultural aspects of those times.

The symbols on the runestones were usually set within a decorated image of a snake or dragon coil and sometimes included other designs. Stone cutters occasionally added more detail to the commissioned text. Runestones also tell of Viking voyages to faraway Byzantium and Baghdad. Many runestones were erected in memory of famous men who died on such journeys. From these stones we have learned about Viking myths, such as the creation of man and the exploits of Viking gods such as Sigurd the dragon-slayer. The most famous runestone from the ninth century is the Rökstone in Östergötland. It has no ornamental design and contains the longest runic text in the world.

The Runic alphabet is of German origin. It has two systems of alphabet: an older system with 24 letters, used from the third to ninth centuries, and a later, simpler alphabet with 16 letters. The golden age of runic writing was in the 11th and 12th centuries, when trade was at its peak.

Opposite: **Like their counterparts in other developed countries, many Swedes read the news over breakfast to keep up with current affairs.**

SVENSKA

The origin of modern *Svenska* is usually dated from the year 1526, when a Swedish translation of the Bible's New Testament was first printed. Standard Swedish, which emerged in the 17th century, is derived mainly from the Svea dialects spoken around Stockholm and Lake Mälaren.

The alphabet that is now used, the Latin alphabet, was introduced in the 13th century through the spread of Christianity. However, the *Svenska* alphabet does not have the letters "w" or "z." Instead it has three other letters, with pronunciation marks: "å," pronounced like the "o" in the English word "for;" "ä," which sounds like the "ai" in the English word

Swedish students doing a class assignment.

"fair;" and "ö," pronounced somewhat like the "u" in the English word "turn." These three unique Swedish letters come at the very end of the *Svenska* alphabet.

The Swedish language became more regulated with the arrival of printing and the production of books in the 15th century. In 1786 King Gustav III founded the Swedish Academy, whose main goal was to improve the "purity, vigour, and majesty" of the language.

In 1836 the academy published a Swedish grammar book. It now publishes two dictionaries: *Svenska Akademiens Ordlista* and *Svenska Akademiens Ordbok* (similar to the Oxford English Dictionary). The 18-member academy, with the motto "Talent and Taste," also awards the Nobel Prize every year.

SPELLING AND PRONUNCIATION

Swedish spelling and pronounciation differ from English convention. For example, the letter "g" can be pronounced with a "g" sound as in *gamla* ("GAHM-lah"), meaning ancient, or with a "y" sound as in *Göteborg* ("YUE-teh-borg"). The letter "j" is pronounced with a "y" sound as in *Ja* ("yah"), meaning yes, and *mjölk* ("myolk"), meaning milk. The letter "k" sounds like "ch," especially when used with the letter "j" or "y," as in *kyckling* ("CHICK-ling"), or chicken, and the Kölen ("CHO-len") mountains.

Pronunciation marks also change the sound of letters. Accent marks indicate which syllable is emphasized as well as the pitch, or tone. There are two tones: high, or acute, and low, or grave.

When learning to write Swedish, it is safer to memorize the correct spelling of a word than try to guess by its pronunciation. For example, there is no simple rule for spelling the "sh" sound in Swedish; "sh" may be left as is or replaced with a "sj" or "sch."

A STANDARD FORM

The standard form of the Swedish language became more widely used than regional dialects in the 20th century for several reasons, such as a central administration and better means of communication and transportation. As people left the countryside for towns and cities, many also left behind their dialects. Standard Swedish gradually spread from the urbanites to the rural populations.

More recently, the mass media and education system have played a major role in spreading the use of a uniform language throughout the country. Swedish children have also learned English in school.

SIMILARITY TO ENGLISH

If you listen closely to a Swede speak, you will probably be able to recognize some words. This is because Swedish and English belong to branches of the same linguistic tree—Germanic. *Svenska* rose out of the North Germanic branch, while English, German, and Dutch developed from the West Germanic branch.

Some Swedish words sound a lot like English: *moder* ("MOH-der"), *fader* ("FAH-der"), *syster* ("SIS-ter"), *broder* ("BROH-der"), *student* ("stu-DENT"), *dörr* ("door"), and *bok* ("book"). Translated into English, these words are mother, father, sister, brother, student, door, and book. Other Swedish words include *tack* ("tahk"), meaning thanks, *tomat* ("toh-MAH"), or tomato, and *frukt* ("froot"), or fruit.

Modern-day Swedish has adopted many foreign words, mainly from Americanized English. Words like "jeans" and "ketchup" are commonly used by Swedes today.

Most Swedes also understand Danish and Norwegian to some degree, since these Scandinavian languages are similar to Swedish.

REGIONAL DIALECTS

There are several regional dialects in Sweden, but these are no longer widely spoken. The Svea dialects came from the provinces in Svealand; the Göta and South Swedish dialects were spoken in the south and the Norrland dialects in the north; the Gotland dialects came from the island of Gotland; and the East Swedish dialects include those spoken in Finland and the Baltic state of Estonia.

Older Swedes, especially those living in more geographically isolated areas in the north, continue to use the dialect of their area. Most young people speak standard Swedish, although with a noticeable regional accent. These accents are so marked that Swedes are able to identify the regional origin of the speaker.

As in many countries, the standard language of Sweden originates from one dialect. Standard Swedish has its roots in a dialect spoken around Lake Mälaren, where the capital, Stockholm, is. Historically, this province was the center of power and economic activity.

An old-fashioned sign shows the true letters peculiar to the Serdish alphabet.

ARTS

SWEDES ENJOY a diverse and developed cultural scene that includes classical expressions such as opera and theater as well as more popular forms such as movies and folk music. With state support, tickets are relatively affordable and facilities easily accessible, making it possible for the average Swede to attend a variety of cultural events.

Cultural tastes in Sweden have changed over the last decade, with more people now choosing popular cultural attractions over traditional ones. Pop and rock music, movies, and television draw a larger following than do opera and theater, for example.

Nevertheless, Swedes are conscious of the need to preserve their heritage. They visit some 300 cultural institutions all over the country, including national museums of art, archeology, natural history, and cultural history; county and municipal museums conserving regional heritage; and folk and other specialized museums.

Left: **Young Swedes enjoy live guitar music.**

Opposite: **An arresting piece from world-famous Swedish glass and crystal manufacturer Kosta Boda.**

A man dressed as a Viking blowing a horn.

THE SOUND OF MUSIC

Although some music Swedes listen to is imported or foreign-influenced, there are still musical forms that are native to Sweden.

FOLK MUSIC Originating in 18th- and 19th-century peasant society, folk music is still sung and enjoyed by Swedes today. Singing games, in which the singers act out the lyrics, are especially popular with children, who learn the songs from an early age.

Originally, Swedish folk songs were sung without musical accompaniment. Peasants sang as they spun wool, did repairs, and made tools on long, cold winter nights. Some of these songs were long ballads that told a story, others were humorous, and still others were religious in nature. The peasants first learned the songs from books and then sang them to their children.

Fiddlers occupied a special place in folk music. They played at weddings and other festivities where there was dancing. Local melodies were handed down from one fiddler to another. Fiddlers were also looked upon as magical figures. There were stories about magic fiddles and fiddlers taught by *Näcken* ("NECK-kehn"), a wicked water spirit. Fiddlers were even thought to be associated with the devil.

Today, the traditions and enthusiasm for folk music are kept alive through clubs, guilds, and competitions. Annual festivals, such as the Music on Lake Siljan Festival for fiddlers, attract many participants and large audiences.

The sound of music

MUSICAL INSTRUMENTS A revival in folk music has renewed interest in folk instruments, especially those with drones that make low-pitched sounds. These include the bowed harp, bagpipe, hurdy-gurdy, Swedish zither, mouth harp, and older keyed fiddles. The keyed fiddle's drone strings give a characteristic tonal sound. The player uses a bow and stops the strings using keys rather than fingers.

Swedish musicians still use old wind instruments such as the clarinet and wooden flute. The cow horn and a wooden trumpet called the *lur* ("LOOR") are used for herding cattle. Herding music, which consists of calls and signals used for communicating with the animals, is thought to be Sweden's oldest surviving domestic musical tradition.

BALLADS Carl Michael Bellman, an 18th-century poet and musician, is considered by many to be the father of the Swedish ballad. His songs, reflecting life on the streets and in the taverns of his time, are still sung today. A Bellman festival is held every year in Stockholm.

In modern times, Evert Taube, often thought of as Sweden's national poet, helped sustain interest in the ballad. Taube was also a visual artist and prose writer who captured the people's imagination. His themes centered on Swedish nature and South America, where he lived for some time in his youth.

SAMI MUSIC The music of the Sami, believed to be the oldest form of music in Europe, reflects their nomadic history and way of life. It is very different from Swedish and other European music. The *jojk* ("yoik") is a spontaneous, improvised song that recalls people or places and evokes related emotions. It is a personal song sung without accompaniment. Musical instruments are rarely used in Sami music.

Carl Michael Bellman's popular drinking songs in the 1760s consisted of borrowed music from the works of others. He revised the tunes where necessary and then performed them, providing accompaniment on his zither.

MOVIES

The Swedish Film Institute is a government agency which supports the production, and distribution, of Swedish films. Swedish films have a reputation abroad of being dark and gloomy. However, the industry does also pay a lot of attention to producing movies for children, many of which are based on well-loved children's stories and characters, such as Astrid Lindgren's Pippi Longstocking.

While most Swedish movies are shown only in Sweden, some have been box office hits in other countries. Ingmar Bergman, for example, made many classics reflecting his view of Sweden. He first achieved international fame with *The Seventh Seal* (1956). This was followed by his Oscar-winning *Wild Strawberries* (1957), *Through a Glass Darkly* (1961), *Cries and Whispers* (1972), and *Fanny and Alexander* (1982).

Thomas Hanzon, Liv Ullman, Lena Endre, and Christer Hensikson at the Cannes Film Festival 2000 to see the premier of their movie *Faithless*, which was based on a script written by Ingmar Bergman.

ART

Art in Sweden is part of everyday life, not just a collection of important paintings housed in a museum. Modern Swedish artists enjoy a strong following, and aspiring painters and sculptors receive training at all levels, from study circles to colleges.

Sweden has its share of internationally well-known painters, such as 20th-century artists Carl Larsson and Anders Zorn. The most well-known Swedish sculptor is Carl Milles. He was very successful in the United States where he worked for several years. Almost every large town in Sweden has a major work by Milles.

Swedish artists have been greatly influenced by European art. But modern artists have also developed their own ideas and created recognizable styles.

Above: **An artist coats toy horses in red paint.**

p97: **A sculpture outside the Royal Dramatic Theater in Stockholm.**

Perhaps the best example of art in daily life is found in Stockholm's subway network. In more than 70 of its 100 stations, colorful murals, sculptures, engravings, and mosaics decorate the ticket booths, track walls, platforms, and ceilings, making the capital's subway network the world's longest art gallery.

Sweden's underground gallery was started in the late 1940s when the subway system was first built. Since then, more than 70 artists have contributed to the colorful "canvas" that makes catching the train everyday such a pleasure. The different works depict and reflect the spirit of each decade. There is a 60-foot (18.3-m) human profile in terazzo, tiles and cobblestones, platform pillars that have been turned into giant trees, fantasy beetles in glass cases, and even a 315-foot- (96-m-) long photo montage of present-day Sweden.

THE GLASSBLOWER'S MAGIC

Glassmaking began in Sweden in the 16th century. Today it is both an industry and an art form. Most of Sweden's glassworks are found in the "Glass District" of Småland. Sweden's master glassblowers work with designers to create "glass art" that is either unique or limited in number. Glassblowing skills are generally passed down from one generation to another.

Many Swedes collect glass and crystal pieces the way people collect paintings, and the designs of certain glass artists are much sought after. Some of Sweden's glassware is world-famous—Orrefors and Kosta Boda manufacture glass art that sells in many countries across the globe.

Some of Sweden's glassworks have revived a local tradition, known as *hyttsill* ("HUIT-seel"). It recalls the days when these glassworks were also meeting places where villagers gathered around the furnaces to gossip and bake herring and potatoes, while a fiddler or accordionist played folk music.

THEATER

The roots of modern Swedish theater can be traced to the 18th century when King Gustavus III opened the doors of his theater to the commoners. Before then, court theaters were available only to the aristocracy. In those days, the actors spoke French instead of Swedish. This was because French was the language of culture in Europe.

Today, Swedes can enjoy a wide range of plays, including classical, modern, children's, and experimental, in the two national theaters —the Opera and the Royal Dramatic Theater in Stockholm.

There are also municipal theaters in other parts of the country that cater to Swedes living outside the capital. The idea of folk theater, or theater for everyone, gave rise to the touring drama company that helped to popularize this art form in Sweden.

The Drottningholm Court Theater, situated in the premises of the residence of the royal family on the outskirts of Stockholm, was built in the 18th century and is believed to be one of the oldest theaters in use today. It stages 30 plays every year and seats only 450 spectators each time. UNESCO declared Drottningholm a World Heritage site in 1992.

AUGUST STRINDBERG TO ASTRID LINDGREN

One of the greatest
Swedish writers
in the 20th century
was Pär Lagerkvist
(1891–1974), who
won a Nobel Prize
in 1951. His
writing during
the 1920s included
love poetry and an
autobiographical
novel, but his best
works involved a
search for vital,
often religious,
values.

The most popular forms of Swedish literature are the novel and poetry. Many Swedish writers have achieved international fame and had their works translated into other languages.

Among the best-known of Sweden's literary figures was August Strindberg (1849–1912), who wrote novels, short stories, poetry, and plays. His works explored the themes of relationships and alienation and were often critical of society. Strindberg won recognition with *The Red Room* (1879) and went on to write several masterpieces, including the psychological drama *The Father* (1887). Some of his plays are still performed all over the world.

One of the most famous authors in Swedish literary history is Selma Lagerlöf, who lived from 1858 to 1940. She won the Nobel Prize for literature in 1909. Although her works have Swedish themes, they have an appeal beyond the country's borders. She wrote novels about country life, weaving in elements of the supernatural.

Lagerlöf wrote her most famous work, *The Wonderful Adventures of Nils*, in 1907. The book follows a boy named Nils as he flies his goose across Sweden. Meant for Swedish schoolchildren, to teach them about Sweden's geography in an entertaining way, it became popular among older readers as well. It has been translated into more than 40 languages and has become a world classic.

A more familiar name is Astrid Lindgren (1907–2002), who wrote many books for children. She mixed fantasy with reality and created mischievous characters that appealed to children. One of the characters she created in 1945, Pippi Longstocking, remains a much-read and well-loved figure across the world. Lindgren did a lot to raise the standard of Swedish literature, and she has a special place in the country's literary tradition.

ALFRED NOBEL AND THE NOBEL PRIZES

Every year on December 10, the prestigious Nobel Prizes are awarded by the king of Sweden in a glittering ceremony at the Concert Hall in Stockholm. These prizes are the legacy of Swedish inventor and industrialist Alfred Nobel, who in his will stipulated that they should be given to those who have "conferred the greatest benefit on mankind." The first Nobel Prize was awarded in 1901.

Reflecting Nobel's interests, the prizes were originally given to people in five areas: physics, chemistry, medicine, literature, and peace. An economics award was added in 1968 in Nobel's memory. All except the peace prize are awarded by Swedish institutions in Stockholm: the Royal Swedish Academy of Sciences for the physics, chemistry, and economics prizes; the Nobel Assembly at the Karolinska Institute for the medicine prize; and the Swedish Academy for the

literature prize. The Norwegian Nobel Committee selects the laureate for the peace prize, which is awarded on the same day as all the other prizes, at the City Hall in Oslo, Norway.

The general process of choosing the winner for each of the Nobel Prizes each year goes something like this: first the committee sends invitations to scientists, academics, and university professors in as many different countries as possible to nominate candidates; with the help of experts, the committee investigates nominations received before the February deadline; the committee then presents its recommendations to the awarding institution, which votes for the final choice; the winner is announced in October; and the prize is awarded at the respective location on December 10 (Alfred Nobel's death anniversary).

Besides establishing the Nobel Prizes, Alfred Nobel also invented dynamite and was a shrewd entrepreneur who set up factories and companies all over the world. Of the 355 inventions Nobel patented during his lifetime, explosives were the most famous.

LEISURE

SWEDES SPEND A LOT OF TIME on leisure activities, especially since the working population enjoys six to 10 weeks of vacation a year. Traditionally, July is the most popular vacation month. Working life seems to come to a stop as most people take their summer vacations.

Most leisure activities take place outdoors, as Swedes enjoy being close to nature and escaping city life as often as they can. Outdoor leisure pursuits enable Swedes to combine two great interests: being with the family and enjoying the warm countryside. Playing some kind of sport is also a popular pastime, for fun and fitness. Sports, whether competitive or friendly, are always taken seriously.

Left: **A shopping street in Stockholm.**

Opposite: **Picking** *lingon*, **a kind of cranberry, is a favorite summer activity with Swedes of all ages.**

SPORTS

Swedish tennis superstars such as Stefan Edberg, Mats Wilander, and the legendary Björn Borg have made their country a force in international tennis, and this success has made the game very popular in Sweden.

Ice hockey is also very popular. Sweden is one of the top five ice hockey nations in the world. Swedes have also distinguished themselves in the prestigious Canada Cup ice hockey competition. Swedish players like Mats Naslund have made a name for themselves and won championship medals while playing in the North American National Hockey League.

Besides dominating in winter sports like alpine skiing and ice skating, Swedes also excel in soccer, table tennis, and rowing. In the 1984 Olympic Games, Sweden's Agneta Andersson won two golds and a silver in the women's kayak rowing events.

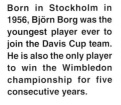

Born in Stockholm in 1956, Björn Borg was the youngest player ever to join the Davis Cup team. He is also the only player to win the Wimbledon championship for five consecutive years.

Mom and dad watch as their little boy splashes in the water.

STARTING YOUNG

Many Swedish children, looking to sports stars such as Borg, Edberg, and Naslund as role models, are anxious to participate in competitive sports even before their teens. In fact, many of Sweden's sports stars began learning their games when they were young.

Junior competitions like the Donald Duck Cup, the biggest tennis tournament for children age 11 to 15, do a lot to give young hopefuls a taste of competition and to spur them to train.

Sweden's sports movement is very organized, coaching thousands of young Swedes. Training programs and facilities help sustain and develop children's interest. In school, sports lessons and clubs and organizations ensure that young talent is developed. Children can also attend "sports high schools," where academic work is combined with training.

Another reason that youth sporting activities are so well developed is that Sweden has nearly half a million unpaid sports coaches who dedicate themselves to training children.

MASS SPORTS

Swedes enjoy doing things together, and this is especially true in sports. Mass races, where participants number in the thousands, are a very old tradition in Sweden. Often, mass events take place over long distances, testing participants' endurance. Several mass sports events attract many people throughout the year.

The most famous mass event is the Vasa Race, where more than 12,000 cross-country skiers compete in a 55-mile (88.5-km) race from Sälen to Mora in the county of Dalarna. Held on the first Sunday every March, the Vasa Race commemorates the escape of Gustav Vasa from the 1520 Bloodbath of Stockholm.

Another mass event is the O-ringen, a five-day orienteering race that attracts as many as 20,000 people who run cross-country using a compass

EVERYMAN'S RIGHT

There is one right that everyone, young and old alike, respects in Sweden. "Everyman's right," or *Allemansrätt* ("AHL-ler-mahns-RAT"), is an ancient tradition that is not written in law. It allows anyone to use any wood, field, or public place, regardless of ownership. It is therefore possible to walk, gather wildflowers and mushrooms, or even camp on private property. There are no laws of trespass. This right, which is treasured by Swedes, is rarely abused. Those who make use of it are careful not to destroy the nature that they have come to appreciate.

and a map for direction.

Church boat races are held every year on Lake Mora as part of the midsummer festival. The race originates from the boat trips people once had to take across the lake from their homes to get to church on the other side. In the races today, the boats carry 20 rowers and passengers who race across the lake dressed in their best clothes.

Other popular events are the Lidingö Race for joggers, the Vansbro Swim, and the Vättern Circuit, a two-day bicycle race along Lake Vättern.

LEARNING ABOUT NATURE

Most recreational activities in Sweden take advantage of the fresh air and rich natural landscape. As more than half of Sweden's land area is wooded, there are plenty of opportunities for nature treks and learning first-hand about the country's flora and fauna.

A frequent feature in school programs are field trips, which supplement classroom learning. Many of these trips teach students about ecology and the natural environment.

Walking is a popular pastime, and families often go off on long treks together during the warmer months. These walks usually turn into nature studies as children are taught to identify different types of wildflowers, trees, and birds. One may spot an elk, a bear, or even a lynx.

There is a network of marked trails all over Sweden. Many of these are dotted with rest stations that allow trekkers to spend the night in some comfort. The most well-known trail is the *Kungsleden*, or Royal Route, in the north; it is more than 300 miles (483 km) long.

In the winter, cross-country skiing replaces walking. This form of skiing is almost second nature to Swedes, although many young people prefer the thrill of downhill skiing.

IT'S SUMMERTIME!

Summer in Sweden is short and active. From the very start of the season, Swedes pack their vacation bags, get into cars, buses, or trains, and head out to the countryside or onto the beaches.

Most families either own a summer house in the countryside or have access to one, where they spend a good part of their summer vacation. Typically, many vacation days are spent picking different types of wild

berries, such as strawberries, raspberries, and blueberries. *Lingon* ("LING-gon"), or cowberry, as well as rose hips and blackberries are the choice of the autumn season. *Lingon* grows all over the country, while another popular berry, the yellow, raspberry-shaped *hjorton* ("YOO-tron"), or cloudberry, is found in the north.

The end of the summer is also the time for picking mushrooms. Walks in the woods turn into mushroom-hunting expeditions, and both young and old search the undergrowth for different types of edible mushrooms, such as chanterelles, cepes, ringed boletuses.

Swedes take berry- and mushroom-picking so seriously that they organize trips to the woods during the picking season. They also attend classes to learn about different kinds of fungi, especially to differentiate the edible species from the inedible ones.

The seaside resort town of Arild on the Kulla Peninsula. Most Swedes living in the city have houses in the country where they spend a relaxed summer.

HEALTHY LIVING

Keeping fit is an important part of Swedish life. Many people jog, cycle, or take part in other sports for both recreation and fitness.

This interest in outdoor activities is promoted by the 23 authorities under the Ministry of Health and Social Affairs. The National Board of Health and Welfare once launched a national campaign to encourage people to exercise regularly, eat right, and avoid tobacco and alcohol.

A number of physical welfare centers were built to encourage the middle-aged and elderly to be more health-conscious, and a wide range of health education programs were provided, from anti-drug to diet. The campaign did instill a consciousness for healthy living and physical well-

Many Swedes enjoy exciting sports such as whitewater rafting.

being. However, only 25 percent of the population exercise regularly, despite the country's wide variety of exercise opportunities, from hiking and skiing to water sports.

In 2001 the National Institute of Public Health launched the "Sweden on the Move" campaign, which focused on increasing physical activity, especially among inactive sections of the population, and on making the outdoors—pathways, cycling tracks, play areas—more exercise-friendly.

FISHING

Fishing is perhaps the favorite noncompetitive sport of Swedes. With thousands of lakes and rivers, home to a variety of fish, such as salmon, perch, and pike, it is not surprising that over 1 million people in Sweden indulge in this pastime.

Boating is a popular summer activity, when Swedes take to the sea, rivers, and lakes. About one-fifth of Swedish households own a boat.

FESTIVALS

MANY SWEDISH FESTIVALS are the product of the country's geography and climate. Due to Sweden's length and northerly location and thus extreme contrasts in weather conditions in different parts of the country and different times of the year, the transition from one season to the next is often marked by some kind of celebration.

History and tradition are other contributing factors to the various festivals. Although many modern Swedes are quite secular in their thinking, religious holidays still form a major part of the festive calendar, and religious traditions continue.

Below: **Two children admire the candles on a Christmas tree.**

Opposite: **Raising the maypole in preparation for the midsummer festival.**

LENT

Swedes still celebrate Shrove Tuesday, the day before Lent, albeit mostly in a secular way. It is customary to eat rich foods before the start of Lent. People in the north eat a hearty meat stew, and those in the south eat *semlor* ("SEHM-lor"), or rolls stuffed with almond paste and whipped cream.

Swedes no longer fast during Lent, not since the Protestant Reformation in the 16th century when Sweden became a Lutheran state.

Many do, however, practice a custom that symbolizes Christ's suffering on his way to his crucifixion at Golgotha—they gather bare twigs and branches of the birch tree and decorate them with brightly colored feathers. These are placed in a vase of water and gradually sprout leaves.

The Feast of Valborg begins with a breakfast of pickled herring and a strong drink. Later in the day, it ends with the lighting of bonfires that can be seen for miles at night.

EASTER

Swedes solemnly observe Easter week, which begins with Palm Sunday. There are no palm processions as in Roman Catholic countries, partly because palms do not grow in Sweden's cold climate. Instead, people place budding varieties of willow branches in vases of water at home or at the office, and the branches sprout leaves by the time Palm Sunday arrives. In some parts of the country, these branches are called palms.

A lighter side of Easter celebrations is in dressing children as "Easter hags" on Maundy Thursday, the eve of Good Friday. The "Easter hags" visit neighbors and give a decorated card, hoping for sweets or a coin in return. In western Sweden, this Easter card or letter is often secretly slipped into the mailbox or under the door. Easter eggs are traditionally eaten the evening before Easter Sunday.

In the western provinces, villages make huge bonfires, with many competing to see who has the biggest bonfire. Fireworks are also let off as part of the festivities. These customs stem from the old superstitious belief that witches came out especially during Easter week, flying off on their broomsticks on Maundy Thursday to meet the devil and flying back the following Saturday. People in those times lit bonfires, shot their firearms into the sky, and painted crosses on their doors, to protect themselves against the witches' black magic.

THE FEAST OF VALBORG

The Feast of Valborg, also known as Walpurgis Night, is a feast not of food but of song. It is the evening when everyone welcomes spring; it is celebrated on April 30 every year, although spring is still weeks away in the north.

One of the most colorful celebrations of the Feast of Valborg is held at Uppsala University, where students gather in the thousands all afternoon. At exactly 3 P.M., they all put on white caps to mark the change in seasons, and they sing traditional songs about spring. This is followed by parties that last until dawn the next day—May Day.

Meanwhile, people elsewhere gather around community bonfires to deliver or hear speeches and to sing a welcome to the return of light. The bonfires have other purposes besides getting rid of trash and witches—they are also supposed to scare away wild animals. Scaring away wild animals is especially important, because cattle are traditionally brought out to pasture on May 1.

May Day sees the start of springtime activities such as picnics and outdoor games. Since it is also Labor Day, it is marked by parades and speeches by labor and political leaders.

A large crowd gathers by a seaside bonfire to celebrate the Feast of Valborg.

Marching bands parade down the streets of Stockholm.

LET'S CELEBRATE!

NATIONAL DAY falls on June 6 in Sweden and is celebrated in schools and most towns with parades, brass bands, and speeches. The king also presents flags to associations and organizations.

National Day is a normal working day in Sweden and the celebrations are relatively quiet compared to those in other countries.

MIDSUMMER is a major festival in Sweden, traditionally celebrated on June 23. Today it is celebrated on the Friday closest to June 23. This is the time when summer days are the longest, and the midnight sun shines all day and night.

On this day, people decorate homes, cars, churches, and other public places with garlands of flowers and leafy branches. Then they gather around a maypole called *majstång* ("MAH-EE-stohng") to dress it with flowers and leaves. They erect the tall, floral-decked cross in the village square or a playground, and young and old alike dance and sing around the decorated maypole. Some places, such as Dalarna in central Sweden, are famous for their midsummer festivities and attract hordes of tourists.

There are several superstitions attached to the midsummer festival. It was believed that the dew that night held special properties and, if collected, could be used to cure illnesses. Certain plants were collected for the same purpose. Those who were single picked a bouquet of seven or nine types of flowers and placed them under their pillow, and they would dream of their future spouse. The future could also be seen by eating "dream herring" and "dream porridge" with plenty of salt in it.

Family and friends sing and dance around the maypole during midsummer festivities.

NEW YEAR'S EVE is a quiet occasion after the Christmas festivities. Many Swedes spend New Year's Eve quietly at home with family or friends. Others may set off fireworks in the streets.

SWEDEN'S FESTIVE CALENDAR

January 1: New Year's Day	June 23: Midsummer
March/April: Easter week	November: All Saints' Day
April 30: Feast of Valborg	November 11: St. Martin's Day
May 1: May (Labor) Day	December: Advent
May/June: Ascension Day	December 13: Lucia Day
June: Pentecost	December 25: Christmas Day
June 6: National Day	December 26: St. Stephen's Day

A Swedish family enjoying a Christmas dinner.

LUCIA DAY AND CHRISTMAS

The most eagerly anticipated festival of the year is Christmas, which lasts from early December to mid-January. The Advent season begins in early December, when people attend special church services. Wreaths, lights, and Christmas trees are put up along streets and in town squares on the first Sunday of December.

At home, families begin the countdown to Christmas by lighting a candle on each of the four Sundays leading up to Christmas. Children have an Advent calendar—cards with date "windows" to be opened each day until Christmas Day.

Lucia Day is celebrated in homes, schools, and communities on December 13, during the Christmas season, in commemoration of St. Lucia of Syracuse. It was traditionally celebrated with plenty of food and drink; according to folk tradition, it was the longest night of the year and both people and animals needed extra nourishment.

At home, Lucia Day begins with a daughter of the family dressing up as St. Lucia, in a long white gown and a crown of candles, and carrying a tray of coffee, saffron buns, ginger snaps, and spicy mulled wine.

In schools, clubs, and community gatherings, a St. Lucia, or "queen of light," is chosen from among the young girls. She leads a procession of attendants dressed in white gowns—girls with glitter in their hair and boys wearing tall, conical hats and carrying a star on a stake. They sing traditional carols and songs.

Christmas Eve is the most festive day of the season. People start the day by decorating the Christmas tree with typical Swedish ornaments: the

Christmas gnome, Noel goat, and ginger cookies in different shapes.

At about 3 P.M., the feasting begins with a traditional *smörgåsbord* ("SMOER-gos-bord") and continues into the evening. After a lavish meal, the children wait for the Christmas gnome, called *tomte* ("TOM-teh"), a Swedish version of Santa Claus. He is expected to appear with presents. It is customary for an adult disguised as the *tomte* to visit the children with gifts. The children get very excited, because by tradition, they have to invite him in for a meal of rice porridge, his favorite food.

The tradition of wrapping Christmas presents is also an important part of the season's festivities.

Church services are held early on Christmas morning, and the rest of the day is spent quietly with the family. Some families continue the merrymaking up to Twelfth Night, or Epiphany, on January 6. The Christmas season ends on Knut's Day on January 13, when the Christmas tree is taken down. Children and their friends take down the tree, have a party, and eat up the edible decorations.

NAMNSDAG

Namnsdag, or Names Day, is almost as important as one's birthday in Sweden. Almost every day of the year is given a name. For example, July 23 is Emma day, and December 11 is Daniel day. In old times, children were given the name of the day they were born on. Everyone with a Swedish name has a day for his or her name and receives greeting cards or flowers from family and friends.

FOOD

THE DAILY DIET IN SWEDEN consists of meat or fish, vegetables, and potatoes. Cheese, a bowl of yogurt, and milk accompany most meals. Swedes are also great coffee drinkers, and the coffee break is considered a national institution.

Certain foods are typical of Swedish cuisine. Although beef and pork are the preferred meats, one can find reindeer and moose meat on some dinner tables. Fish is a favorite food, and there are many ways of preparing fish. The two most common types of fish in the Swedish diet are salmon and herring; a typical Swedish meal would not be complete without one of these.

Above: **Fresh fruit on sale at a market in Stockholm.**

Opposite: **A Swedish man savors a feast of eel on his yacht.**

Although only a small proportion of resources is used in farming, Sweden is agriculturally self-sufficient. Prices of imported foods are higher than in most other European countries partly because of Sweden's high import taxes. Although few foreign foods find their way into the family's daily meals, this is slowly changing with the influence of immigrants.

MEALTIMES

Breakfast is usually a meal of cereal, bread, butter, and cheese, with coffee, tea, fermented milk, or yogurt. The main meal of the day, called *middag* ("MID-dahg"), is traditionally served at 4 P.M., and a supper of coffee and cakes or a cold buffet after 8 P.M.

However, these mealtimes are not practical for working people, who instead have a light lunch at 12:30 P.M. A *smörgås* ("SMOER-gos"), or open-faced sandwich, is the most popular lunchtime food. People usually have dinner after coming home from the office. This includes a main dish of meat or fish with potatoes, and cheese or fruit.

SEASONAL FOOD

A change of seasons brings changes in the food consumed. Easter food is eaten at the end of a long winter, with eggs cooked in different ways, roast lamb, and *semlor.* A roll made from wheat flour and filled with marzipan and whipped cream, *semlor* are usually eaten before Lent, with a bowl of hot milk and cinnamon.

Cold foods are eaten in the summer. Some people only have a bowl of fermented milk for dinner. The end of summer is also the mushroom-eating season.

All kinds of berries are picked and eaten in large quantities in the summer. The *lingon,* a type of cranberry, a typical Swedish berry, is a red, bittersweet fruit often made into a jam that the Swedish eat with almost everything, from pancakes to meatballs. The *hjorton,* or cloudberry, is a tiny gold-colored fruit that grows in the north and is a favorite of many.

The crayfish season starts on the second Wednesday in August each year. Groups of friends and family members gather to eat crayfish boiled in salted water and seasoned with flowering dill. Only bread and a spiced cheese are eaten with crayfish, which is washed down with beer. Homes are cheerily decorated with lanterns, and everyone wears funny hats, such as paper crayfish with claws sticking out like horns, and paper bibs.

An egg-packing plant in Västergötland.

Hot, robust meals like stews are preferred in the winter. A heavy pea soup with salted pork is traditionally served on Thursday at this time of the year. This meal is eaten with pancakes and jam. Other popular winter dishes include stewed brown beans with fried pork, and beef stew served with *lingon* jam, pickled beetroot, and cucumber.

TABLE MANNERS

Swedes like things well-ordered. This is true even in the social sphere, where rules of behavior are kept. These rules apply at formal dinners as well as casual meals. For example, Swedes are always punctual; it is considered bad manners to be late. Many arrive early and wait to present themselves at the door at the appointed time. It is customary to bring a gift, perhaps a box of chocolates or even a bouquet of flowers, for the hostess.

Friends gathered for a lobster party.

To start the meal, the host gives a short speech and then raises his glass for the first *skål* ("skohl"), or toast, to welcome his guests. The guests are expected to reply with the word *skål* and then establish eye contact with fellow guests, especially those sitting across from or closest to them. Eye contact is reestablished after a sip is taken.

At a formal dinner, guests are not supposed to drink their wine unless in a *skål.* They either have to offer a toast or wait to be toasted. At an informal meal, the host will usually announce that "drinking is free," which means that guests are allowed to drink without having to *skål* one another. A popular story explains the origin of this custom from the time of the Vikings. They trusted no one and thus made toasts while keeping an eye out for any unpleasant surprises (like a stab in the heart).

Toward the end of the meal, the guest on the left of the hostess is expected to give a short speech of thanks on behalf of the others. Children are taught at an early age to thank their hostess by saying "*Tack för maten,*" ("tahk fur MAH-tehn"), meaning "Thank you for the food." Guests are expected to give a phone call or send a note the next day to thank the hostess for her hospitality.

TRADITIONAL COOKING METHODS

A lot of Swedish food is still prepared using traditional methods. A good example is the preparation of fish, a staple in the diet.

In the old days, the irregular supply of fish and the difficulty of fishing during the winter in the frozen north gave rise to different methods of preserving fish. It is not surprising to still find a number of dishes that include salted, dried, or smoked fish.

Gravad lax ("GRAH-vahd lax"), or marinated salmon, is one of the most well-known Swedish dishes. The method of marinating, or *gravning* ("GRAHV-ning"), is one of the oldest curing methods. *Gravning* comes from the word *begrava* ("beh-GRAH-vah"), which means bury. The old method was to bury the fish after salting it lightly to preserve it, because salt was an expensive commodity. This method of preparation also gave

Right: **Friends enjoy traditional Swedish cuisine, including seasonal crayfish.**

Opposite: **A Swedish woman carrying rounds of cheese.**

rise to fermentation, another old Swedish preservation method.

Fish is no longer buried or fermented to marinate. The fish is simply rubbed with salt, sugar, and herbs and left to cure for a day or two in the refrigerator.

Meat was also dried and salted in the old days. *Spicken* ("SPICK-kehn"), another word with ancient roots, referred to the method of stretching out meat or fish on wooden sticks to dry in the sun, after which it would be salted. Today, meats are still sun-dried and salted, but fish is just salted.

One area where tradition prevails is in the baking of *knäckebröd* ("ker-NECK-keh-brod"), or crispbread, sometimes called hard bread. Most varieties of this unleavened, wholemeal rye bread are machine-made, although some are baked in old-fashioned wooden stoves in certain areas such as Dalarna. This large, thin, round bread had a hole in its center, through which a pole would be threaded and hung above the family's wooden stove. This was the traditional method of storing crispbread.

Originally, crispbread was coarse in texture, dry, and durable due to the high temperature at which it was baked. Today, however, it is possible to find a variety of crispbreads with different textures and hardness.

THE SMÖRGÅSBORD

The best example of Sweden's food heritage is found in the *smörgåsbord*, which means "open sandwich table." The *smörgåsbord* is a buffet-style meal of cold and hot dishes where diners help themselves to the great variety of excellent Swedish cuisine.

The practice of laying out different dishes on the table is said to have started in the 16th century. *Smörgåsbord* is said to be descended from the *brännvin* ("BRAN-vin") table, where the first course of a banquet was laid on a separate table. Guests stood for this course of *brännvin* (vodka made from corn or potatoes), herring, anchovies, bread, and strong cheese. They would then be seated for the main meal.

Over the centuries, more dishes were added to the first course until its peak in the 19th century, when it began to be served in homes and restaurants. Today, the *smörgåsbord* is no longer the first course but the whole meal for Swedes. Since they no longer have the time to prepare the same enormous amount and variety of food, they offer scaled-down versions when entertaining at home. Nevertheless, on special occasions and especially at Christmas, they do still celebrate with a laden table that recalls their heritage.

In a traditional *smörgåsbord*, the table is piled with as many as 40 dishes, all laid out together. However, to truly appreciate the meal, diners have the *smörgåsbord* in five courses. The general rule is to serve fish dishes first, then cold meats and salads, then hot dishes, and finally desserts. Bread and butter are served throughout the first four courses.

In the first course, people work up an appetite with a variety of herrings prepared in different ways (salted, pickled, marinated; in cream sauce, dill, sherry), and strong, hard cheeses, accompanied by crispbread.

The second course offers fish such as mackerel and cod, with salmon being the highlight.

Cold meats make up the third course; this includes delicacies such as dried leg of mutton and smoked reindeer and is accompanied by salads and pickled vegetables. In the fourth course, hot dishes are served, including meatballs, a favorite of Swedish children, and Jansson's Temptation, a baked dish of potatoes and anchovies.

The fifth course completes the meal with desserts: creamy cakes, Swedish apple pies, and fresh fruit.

Although *smörgåsbord* meals are found all over Sweden, Skåne province is especially famous for its *smörgåsbord*.

Above: **A Swedish chef holds out a tantalizing plate of cured salmon.**

Opposite: **The longest *smörgåsbord* in the world, at Stockholm's King Street.**

A traditional midsummer's day lunch of *matjesill* ("MAHT-yeh-sill"), or sweet pickled herring with sour cream and chopped chives. Besides beer, a small glass of *snaps* is served.

A RECIPE FOR CHRISTMAS RICE PORRIDGE

1$^1/_3$ cups water
1 teaspoon salt
1 tablespoon butter
1 cinnamon stick
$^2/_3$ cup round-grained rice
2 $^2/_3$ cups milk
Sugar and cinnamon to taste

Boil water with salt, butter, and cinnamon stick. Add rice, cover and cook on low heat for 10 minutes. Add milk and cook, uncovered, on very low heat for another 30 minutes until the milk is absorbed. Stir continuously so that the porridge does not burn. Add sugar and cinnamon to taste, and serve.

SNAPS

No *smörgåsbord* is complete without *snaps* ("snahps"), or aquavit, drunk by the glassful. *Snaps* glasses are relatively small, but even a small quantity packs a powerful punch. *Snaps* is made from potatoes or barley and varies a great deal in flavor. Different types of herbs and spices, such as caraway seeds, cumin, and dill, are used in the flavoring. There are at least 20 flavored *snaps* to choose from.

The importance of *snaps* in Swedish drinking tradition is found in the drinking ritual. There is no ritual in the drinking of beer, which is also drunk with the *smörgåsbord*. But for *snaps*, it is very important to raise glasses for a mutual toast before drinking, after which either the *skål* rule applies or guests are allowed to drink at their liberty. According to an old tradition, husbands are expected to *skål* their wives. If they forget, their wives can demand a pair of stockings as compensation.

What Swedes really enjoy most is a song before gulping down the *snaps*. These traditional drinking songs are sung by everyone and end almost in a shout. There are countless songs, some with witty lyrics and full of puns. Different occasions call for different songs, although they can be sung in any season.

FESTIVAL FOOD

The most important date in the Swedish calendar is Christmas. Early in December, the smell of spicy Christmas food being baked wafts through the air. Even those who rarely bake try their hand at turning out ginger snaps and saffron buns.

On Lucia Day, December 13, people in the office gather in their coffee corners, sipping spiced, mulled wine and eating ginger snaps and saffron buns. The wine is a mixture of red wine and *snaps*, spiced with cinnamon, cloves, and cardamom. This spicy, sweet mix is served piping hot with raisins and almonds. Ginger snaps are thin, crisp, spice cookies that are eaten year round and especially during Christmas.

Children have their share of the festive goodies, except the hot wine; they enjoy hot chocolate instead.

A traditional Christmas spread. Christmas food is highly spiced, typically with cloves, ginger, allspice, and bay leaves. To many Swedes, the spicy smells from the cooking and baking are as much a part of Christmas as the other rituals of this festival.

The *smörgåsbord* eaten on the afternoon of Christmas Eve presents a slightly different spread from that eaten during the rest of the year. It has sweet-sour red cabbage, mustard-glazed baked ham, sausages, and pickled pigs' feet. Certain dishes commemorate old times. For example, "Dip in the Pot" recalls the time when poor farm hands were invited to dip their bread in the broth where ham and other meats had been boiled. That was the closest they got to tasting the ham. Today, a special herb-flavored bread is dipped in this tasty broth.

Another winter dish is *lutfisk* ("LOOT-fisk"), a salted and dried codfish soaked in lye from December 9 so that it is ready on Christmas Day.

Young children in Sweden leave a bowl of rice porridge for the Christmas *tomte* to eat when he comes to visit them. This thick porridge is eaten as a dessert on Christmas Eve. Rice is boiled with milk and served with sugar and cinnamon. Sometimes a single almond is added. It is believed that a single person who gets the almond in his or her portion will be married within the year.

TRADITIONAL SWEDISH MEATBALLS

This recipe makes four servings. Serve with sauteed vegetables and fresh bread.

6 tablespoons butter or margarine
1 chopped onion
1 cup dried bread crumbs
1 cup evaporated milk
1½ pounds (680 g) ground beef
1 beaten egg

1 teaspoon salt
¼ teaspoon ground black pepper
1 pinch dried parsley
1½ teaspoons all-purpose flour
1 tablespoon tomato sauce
Ground nutmeg to taste

Melt 3 tablespoons of the butter in a large skillet over medium heat. Add the onion, and saute for 5 to 10 minutes, or until tender. In a separate bowl, combine the bread crumbs with 2 tablespoons of the milk and stir, allowing the crumbs to absorb the milk. Add the beef, egg, salt, pepper, and parsley to taste. Mix well and form into golfball-sized meatballs. Heat the remaining butter in the same skillet over medium heat, and add the meatballs. Carefully shake the skillet to turn the meatballs. Saute for 10 to 15 minutes, or until the meatballs are browned on all sides. Transfer the meatballs to a serving platter, leaving the liquid in the skillet. Add the flour to the skillet, and stir until smooth. Then gradually add the milk, tomato sauce, and nutmeg to taste, stirring until the mixture is warmed, smooth, and creamy. Strain over the meatballs.

SWEDISH APPLECAKE

This recipe makes 12 servings.

2½ cups fine dry bread crumbs
1¼ cups firmly packed light brown sugar
1 tablespoon ground cinnamon
2½ pounds (930 g) pie-sliced apples

16 ounces (2 cups) canned or jarred applesauce
Juice of 1½ lemons
½ cup (250 ml) butter
Custard sauce, ice cream, or whipped cream

Combine the bread crumbs, sugar, and cinnamon in a mixing bowl. In another bowl, mix the apples, applesauce, and lemon juice. Butter a 13 x 9 inch (5.2 x 3.6 cm) baking pan or a round 4-inch (10-cm) diameter pie tin. Place alternate layers of crumbs and apple mixture in the pan, starting and ending with a good layer of bread crumbs. Dot each layer of crumbs with butter. Bake the mixture in a preheated oven at 400ºF (204ºC) for 45 minutes. Serve warm or cold with custard sauce, ice cream, or whipped cream.

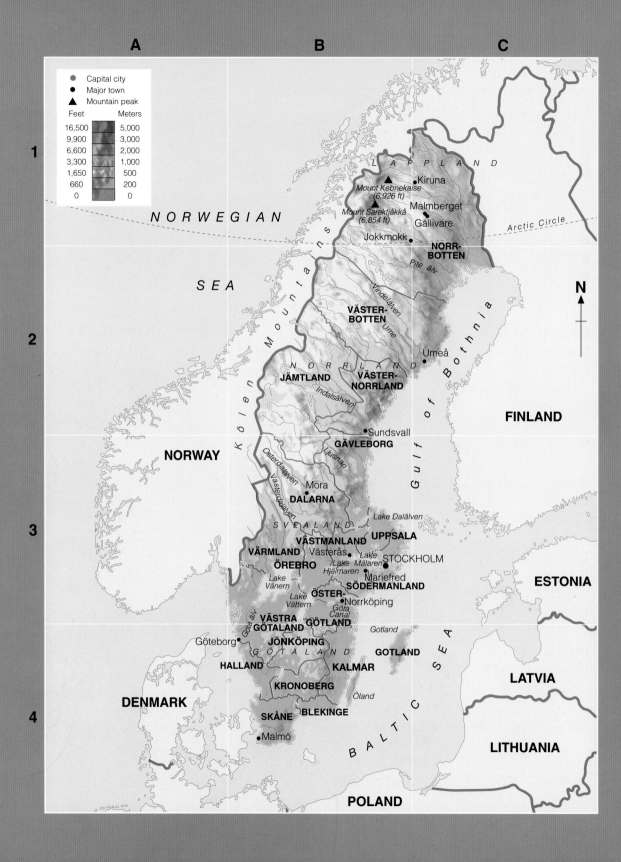

A | B | C

1

2

3

4

Capital city
Major town
Mountain peak

Feet	Meters
16,500	5,000
9,900	3,000
6,600	2,000
3,300	1,000
1,650	500
660	200
0	0

N O R W E G I A N

S E A

L A P P L A N D

Mount Kebnekaise
(6,926 ft)
•Kiruna

Mount Sarektjåkkå
(6,854 ft)
Malmberget
•Gällivare

Jokkmokk•
**NORR-
BOTTEN**

Arctic Circle

Pite älv

Vindelälven

**VÄSTER-
BOTTEN**

Ume

N

N O R R L A N D

•Umeå

JÄMTLAND

**VÄSTER-
NORRLAND**

Indalsälven

NORWAY

Kölen Mountains

Gulf of Bothnia

FINLAND

•Sundsvall

GÄVLEBORG

Ljusnan

Österdalälven

•Mora

DALARNA

Västerdalälven

S V E A L A N D

Lake Dalälven

VÄSTMANLAND

UPPSALA

VÄRMLAND   Västerås•
ÖREBRO   *Lake
Hjälmaren*   *Lake
Mälaren*   STOCKHOLM

*Lake
Vänern*

Mariefred•
SÖDERMANLAND

ÖSTER-
*Lake
Vättern*   **GÖTLAND** •Norrköping

*Göta
Canal*

**VÄSTRA
GÖTALAND**   **GÖTLAND**

Göta älv

Göteborg•

JÖNKÖPING

Gotland

G Ö T A L A N D

GOTLAND

HALLAND

KALMAR

KRONOBERG

Öland

DENMARK

SKÅNE   **BLEKINGE**

Malmö•

ESTONIA

*B A L T I C
S E A*

LATVIA

LITHUANIA

POLAND

MAP OF SWEDEN

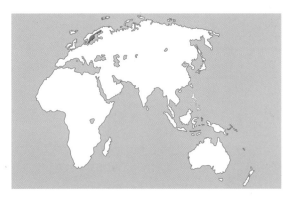

ECONOMIC SWEDEN

Services

 Airport

 Port

Manufacturing

 Vehicles

Natural Resources

 Crystal

 Hydroelectricity

 Iron and Steel

 Nuclear Reactor

 Timber

Farming

 Reindeer

 Vegetables

 Wheat

ABOUT
THE ECONOMY

GDP
$197 billion (2000)
Per capita: $22,200

NATURAL RESOURCES
Metals (zinc, iron ore, lead, copper, silver), timber, uranium, hydropower

GDP SECTORS
Agriculture 2.2 percent, industry 27.9 percent, services 69.9 percent

LAND USE
Arable land 7 percent, forests and woodland 68 percent, permanent pastures 1 percent, other 24 percent

AGRICULTURAL PRODUCTS
Grain, sugar beets, potatoes, meat, milk

INDUSTRIAL PRODUCTS
Iron and steel, armaments, television parts, wood pulp and paper, processed foods, motor vehicles

CURRENCY
Swedish krona (SEK)
1 krona = 100 öre
USD 1 = SEK 9.2674 (October 2002)
Notes: 20, 50, 100, 500, 1000 krona
Coins: 50 öre; 1, 5, 10 krona

INFLATION RATE
1.2 percent (2000)

LABOR FORCE
4.4 million

LABOR DISTRIBUTION
Agriculture 2 percent, industry 24 percent, services 74 percent

UNEMPLOYMENT RATE
6 percent (2000)

MAJOR TRADE PARTNERS
European Union (Germany, United Kingdom, Denmark, Finland, France), United States, Norway

TOTAL EXPORTS
$95.5 billion (2000)

TOTAL IMPORTS
$80 billion (2000)

PORTS AND HARBORS
Gävle, Göteborg, Halmstad, Hälsingborg, Helsingborg, Kalmar, Karlshamn, Malmö, Solvesborg, Stockholm, Sundsvall

AIRPORTS
255 total; 147 with paved runways (2000)

COMMUNICATIONS MEDIA
Telephone: 6.017 million operating main lines; 3.835 million mobile cellular phones (1998)
Internet: 29 service providers (ISPs); 4.5 million users (2000)

CULTURAL SWEDEN

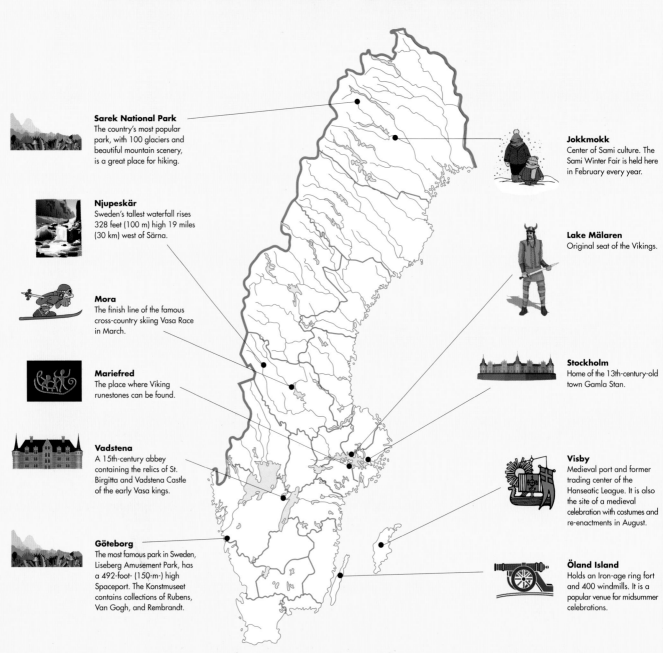

Sarek National Park
The country's most popular park, with 100 glaciers and beautiful mountain scenery, is a great place for hiking.

Njupeskär
Sweden's tallest waterfall rises 328 feet (100 m) high 19 miles (30 km) west of Särna.

Mora
The finish line of the famous cross-country skiing Vasa Race in March.

Mariefred
The place where Viking runestones can be found.

Vadstena
A 15th-century abbey containing the relics of St. Birgitta and Vadstena Castle of the early Vasa kings.

Göteborg
The most famous park in Sweden, Liseberg Amusement Park, has a 492-foot- (150-m-) high Spaceport. The Konstmuseet contains collections of Rubens, Van Gogh, and Rembrandt.

Jokkmokk
Center of Sami culture. The Sami Winter Fair is held here in February every year.

Lake Mälaren
Original seat of the Vikings.

Stockholm
Home of the 13th-century-old town Gamla Stan.

Visby
Medieval port and former trading center of the Hanseatic League. It is also the site of a medieval celebration with costumes and re-enactments in August.

Öland Island
Holds an Iron-age ring fort and 400 windmills. It is a popular venue for midsummer celebrations.

ABOUT THE CULTURE

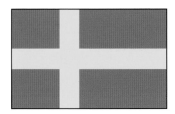

OFFICIAL NAME
Kingdom of Sweden

NATIONAL FLAG
Light blue background with a yellow cross that extends to the edges; the vertical axis of the cross is nearer the hoist in the style of the Danish flag.

NATIONAL ANTHEM
Du gamla, du fria (Thou ancient, thou free). Words by R. Dybeck set to folk music.

CAPITAL
Stockholm

ADMINISTRATIVE DIVISIONS (COUNTIES)
Blekinge, Dalarna, Gävleborg, Gotland, Halland, Jämtland, Jönköping, Kalmar, Kronoberg, Norrbotten, Örebro, Östergötland, Skåne, Södermanland, Stockholm, Uppsala, Värmland, Västerbotten, Västernorrland, Västmanland, Västra Götaland

POPULATION
8,875,053 (July 2001)

POPULATION GROWTH RATE
0.02 percent (2001)

AGE STRUCTURE
14 years and below: 18 percent; 15 to 64 years: 65 percent; 65 years and over: 17 percent

LIFE EXPECTANCY
80 years (2001)

ETHNIC GROUPS
Indigenous Swedish, Finnish, Sami; immigrant Danish, Greek, Norwegian, Turkish, Yugoslav

RELIGIOUS GROUPS
Lutheran majority, Roman Catholic, Orthodox, Baptist, Muslim, Jewish, Buddhist

OFFICIAL LANGUAGE
Swedish

LITERACY RATE
99 percent

NATIONAL HOLIDAY
National Day (June 6)

LEADERS IN POLITICS
Gustav Vasa (1523–60)—first Vasa king; founded Sweden's monarchy and state religion
Gustavus II Adolphus (1611–32)—grandson of Gustav Vasa; expanded Sweden's frontiers in the Baltic and Poland
Jean-Baptiste Bernadotte (1818–44)—King Karl XIV; brought Norway under Swedish control
Dag Hammarskjöld (1905–61)—former Secretary-General to the United Nations (1953–61)
Olof Palme (1927–86)—former Social Democrat prime minister (1972–76, 1982–86); assassinated

TIME LINE

IN SWEDEN	IN THE WORLD

12,000 B.C.
Stone Age people settle Scandinavia.

753 B.C.
Rome is founded.

116–17 B.C.
The Roman empire reaches its greatest extent, under Emperor Trajan (98–17).

A.D. 400s
First Swedish state, Kingdom of the Svear, is established, centered in Uppland.

A.D. 550
Gotlanders put themselves under the protection of the Swedish king.

A.D. 600
Height of Mayan civilization

A.D. 800
Beginning of the Viking Era

1000
The Chinese perfect gunpowder and begin to use it in warfare.

1523
Gustav Eriksson Vasa is elected King of Sweden; Stockholm becomes the capital city.

1530
Beginning of trans-Atlantic slave trade organized by the Portuguese in Africa

1544
Vasa declares hereditary monarchy and Lutheranism as state religion.

1558–1603
Reign of Elizabeth I of England

1620
Pilgrim Fathers sail the *Mayflower* to America.

1776
U.S. Declaration of Independence

1789–99
French Revolution

1818
Jean-Baptiste Bernadotte is crowned King Karl XIV.

1861
U.S. Civil War begins.

1869
The Suez Canal is opened.

1875
A common basis of currency is established with Denmark and Norway.

1914
War in Europe begins; Sweden proclaims complete neutrality.

1914
World War I begins.

IN SWEDEN	IN THE WORLD
	1939 World War II begins.
1944 All trade with Germany ceases.	**1945** The United States drops atomic bombs on Hiroshima and Nagasaki.
1946 Sweden joins the United Nations.	**1949** North Atlantic Treaty Organization (NATO) is formed.
	1957 Russians launch Sputnik.
1965 Queen Louise dies peacefully. Voting age is lowered from 21 to 20.	**1966–69** Chinese Cultural Revolution
1973 Carl XVI Gustaf becomes king.	
1975 Swedish parliament opens its 75th session. Under the new constitution, the king is a figurehead with no real powers.	
1982 Olof Palme is sworn in as prime minister.	
1986 Palme is shot dead in Stockholm.	**1986** Nuclear power disaster at Chernobyl in Ukraine
1991 Parliament elects Carl Bildt as the first conservative prime minister in 63 years.	**1991** Break-up of the Soviet Union
1995 Sweden joins the European Union. Visby enters the UNESCO World Heritage list.	**1997** Hong Kong is returned to China.
1998 Göran Persson is elected prime minister.	
2001 Persson begins Sweden's six-month presidency of the European Union.	**2001** World population surpasses 6 billion.

GLOSSARY

daghem ("DAHG-hem")
A day-care center.

Götaland ("YUE-tah-land")
The region known as southern Sweden.

gravad lax ("GRAH-vahd lax")
Marinated salmon.

gymnasium ("gim-NAH-sium")
Senior high school.

jojk ("yoik")
A spontaneous, improvised style of singing.

knäckebröd ("ker-NECK-keh-brod")
Crispbread, sometimes called hard bread.

lappkok ("LAHP-shehk")
Reindeer marrow bone and liver broth.

lingon ("LING-on")
A round, red berry, also called cowberry.

lur ("LOOR")
A wooden trumpet used for herding cattle.

majstång ("MAH-EE-stohng")
The maypole people dance around at midsummer.

matjesill ("MAHT-yeh-sill")
Sweet pickled herring.

middag ("MID-dahg")
The main meal of the day, served at 4 P.M.

Norrland ("NOR-land")
The northern region of Sweden.

ombudsman
An official investigating complaints against public authorities.

Riksdag ("RICKS-dahg")
Sweden's parliament.

semlor ("sehm-LOH")
A stuffed roll, usually eaten during Lent.

skål ("skohl")
A toast to one's health.

smörgåsbord ("SMOER-gos-bord")
A buffet of Swedish specialties.

snäll ("snell")
To be pleasant and considerate to elders.

snaps ("snahps")
Aquavit, a Swedish liquor made from fermented potatoes and barley.

strömming ("STROHM-ming")
A species of herring from the Baltic Sea.

Svealand ("SVEE-ah-land")
The region in central Sweden.

tomte ("TOM-teh")
Sweden's Santa Claus, a Christmas gnome who appears with presents

FURTHER READING

BOOKS

Boraas, Tracy. *Sweden.* Countries and Cultures Series. Minnesota: Bridgestone Books, 2002.

Butler, Robbie. *Sweden.* Nations of the World Series. New Jersey: Raintree Steck-Vaughn, 2000.

Lagerlöf, Selma. *The Wonderful Adventures of Nils.* Iowa: Penfield Books, 2000.

Lagerlöf, Selma. *The Further Adventures of Nils Holgersson.* Iowa: Penfield Books, 2000.

Lindgren, Astrid Ericsson. *Pippi Longstocking.* New York: Puffin Books, 1997. (There are many Pippi books and editions to choose from.)

MacGregor, Roy. *Kidnapped in Sweden (Screech Owls #5).* Toronto: McClelland and Steward, 1996. (Part of the series on young hockey players' adventures around the world)

McDonald, Jo. *Sweden in Pictures.* Minneapolis: Lerner Publications Company, 1998.

WEBSITES

Central Intelligence Agency World Factbook (select "Sweden" from the country list). www.cia.gov/cia/publications/factbook

Children's ombudsman. www.bo.se

Lonely Planet World Guide: Destination Sweden. www.lonelyplanet.com/destinations/europe/sweden

Nobel e-Museum. www.nobel.se/nobel/alfred-nobel/index.html

The Royal Court of Sweden. www.royalcourt.se/net/Royal+Court

Smorgasbord: The Shortcut to Sweden. www.sverigeturism.se/smorgasbord

The Swedish Government. www.sweden.gov.se

The Swedish Parliament. www.riksdagen.se/index_en.asp

MUSIC

Folk Music from Sweden. Various Artists. Arc Music, 2001.

Music from Sweden. Blekinge Spelmansforbund. Arc Music, 2002.

Power from the North: Sweden Rocks the Rock. Various Artists. Digital Dimension, 2000.

You can also check out music by Abba, Ace of Base, The Cardigans, and Covenant.

VIDEOS

Families of Sweden. San Pedro, California: Master Communication, 1998.

Pippi Longstocking. Swedish original (1973) with Inger Nilsson, dubbed in English. New York: Vid-America.

Pippi Longstocking. Animated. Atlanta: Turner Home Video, 1997.

Royal Families of the World: Great Britain, Sweden, Netherlands, Belgium. California: Goldhill Home Media, 1999.

Scandinavia: Denmark, Sweden and Norway. With Rick Steves. Chicago, Illinois: Questar Inc., 1999.

BIBLIOGRAPHY

Dinan, Desmond (editor). *Encyclopedia of the European Union*. Boulder and London: Lynne Rienner Publishers, 2000.

Turner, Barry (editor). *The Statesman's Yearbook 2002*. Hampshire, England. Palgrave Publishers, 2001.

Europa World Yearbook 2000.

Central Intelligence Agency World Factbook. www.cia.gov/cia/publications/factbook

Chronology of Sweden. www.islandnet.com/~kpolsson/swedhis

Food and Agriculture Organization of the United Nations. www.fao.org

United Nations Environmental Network. www.unep.net

INDEX